COLOR IN SMALL SPACES

Palettes and Styles to Fit Your Home

Brenda Grant-Hays, ID, NCIDQ
and
Kimberly A. Mikula, IIDA, NCIDQ

McGraw-Hill

New York   Chicago   San Francisco   Lisbon   London   Madrid
Mexico City   Milan   New Delhi   San Juan   Seoul
Singapore   Sydney   Toronto

The McGraw-Hill Companies

Cataloging-in-Publication Data is on file with the Library of Congress

1 2 3 4 5 6 7 8 9 0 PUR/PUR 0 9 8 7 6 5 4 3 2 1

ISBN 0-07-138313-1

The sponsoring editor for this book was Cary Sullivan, the editing liaison was Steven Melvin, and the production supervisor was Sherri Souffrance. It was set in Candida by North Market Street Graphics.

Printed in China by Print Vision

McGraw-Hill books are available at special quantity discounts to use as premiums and sales promotions, or for use in corporate training programs. For more information, please write to the Director of Special Sales, McGraw-Hill, 2 Penn Plaza, New York, NY 10121-2298. Or contact your local bookstore.

This book is printed on acid-free stock.

To our spouses, Michael Hays and Joe Mikula; to our families, Bob and Ruthann Tile, the late Gladys and Raymond Grant, Ryan, Hannah, Sheila, Patti, Michelle, and their families; and to our many soul sisters, whose patience, encouragement, and support were invaluable and made a difficult process a little easier.

"This book clearly shows how the effective use of color is an integral part of fine design. It is a 'must-have' book for anyone interested in creating unique, exciting spaces in their home."

—Michael Payne, host and interior designer of HGTV's
Designing for the Sexes

"*Color in Small Spaces* deftly articulates the formidable power of color as a design element. Through a very specific focus, the authors expertly guide readers through a spectrum of solutions that consider the aesthetic and functional values of color. Engaging, informative narrative in tandem with photos, floor plans, and graphics that illustrate and define the work of highly regarded design professionals; this volume goes well beyond a 'how-to.' *Color in Small Spaces* is a valuable reference tool for consumers, design students, seasoned professionals—anyone enhancing the built environment through the use of one of its most powerful components."

—Cheryl S. Durst, Hon. IIDA, Executive Vice President/CEO,
International Interior Design Association

CONTENTS

INTRODUCTION

Color. Radiant energy, each color having its own distinct wavelength. We can explain it scientifically. We can theorize about our physiological responses to it. Ultimately, some people will be comfortable using it. Some will not. Color is one of the many ways we showcase our individuality, whether it is in the color of clothes we wear, the color of car we drive, or the colors with which we surround ourselves in our homes.

In the pages that follow, we will introduce you to the principles and theory of color. If you are living in or designing a home or apartment that is small in size, the use of color becomes even more precise. We will discuss why we react to some colors the way we do and how light affects its use. As we explore the use of color in our environments, we will lead you by the hand through various applications and uses in spaces around the globe. The expertise of the designers and architects whose work is showcased in these pages will speak to both established color application and beyond. Most will be small spaces, some will not, but all will lend valuable insight and thought regarding how to use color well. Whether you are a seasoned designer or simply want to learn more about it, our straightforward approach will help you on your way.

ACKNOWLEDGMENTS

We would like to acknowledge the people who have provided assistance and editorial support for this book since its inception. The book has developed as a result of the efforts of many people and their valuable contributions. We would like to thank Cary Sullivan, Cathy Markoff, and Scott Grillo for their editorial guidance throughout the developmental editing as well as the many hands at McGraw-Hill who helped with this process. We would also like to acknowledge the support of Wendy Lochner, who helped launch the idea of this book. Additionally we would like to thank the professionals at North Market Street Graphics for their efforts above and beyond with the pages in this book. Thank you to Christine Furry, Lainey Harding, Anne DeLozier, and Jan Bedger for your support! Thanks to IIDA and ASID, as these professional organizations continue to be supportive to all interior designers. Last, our gratitude rests with the many talented designers and photographers who have contributed photographs of their exceptional work to this project. Without their talents, this book could not have been completed.

PART 1
The Basics: Color and Materials

CHAPTER 1
Principles of Color

We've used color throughout the ages at times out of need, desire, availability, and status. The need, in many respects, was to distinguish ourselves from other mammals. The desire was to change our surroundings to either differentiate from or blend in with our surroundings. In either instance, we used color. The availability of color was connected to our geography and the pigments indigenous to that place and time. If we lived near salt water, for example, we could obtain the pigments of indigo and violet from squid ink. Certain flowers produced stamens with intense reds such as saffron. Red and blue clays from the earth gave way to rich colors and textures in pottery and tile. Colors that were most rare and difficult to obtain became the colors of status and were reserved for the wealthiest and noblest.

Eventually, the availability and variety of color became so pervasive that we needed to establish a system that would enable anyone to understand how to use color well. Although there's more than one color system, the foundation of all is the *color spectrum*, which is what we see when we look at rainbows and prisms.

Our intent in this chapter is not to delve into an exhaustive analysis of color history and systems, but rather to approach the fundamentals of color as they apply to us for practical application. We'll look at what color is and why we see the colors we see, and we'll introduce the basic color wheels and present the Munsell color system. In addition, we'll examine the basics of color palettes with primary colors, monochromatic colors, and complementary colors. We'll also explore contrasts, light shades, color saturation and intensity, natural color palettes, and how to incorporate natural materials.

Light and Color

Science explains our perception of color as follows: Light is a form of radiant energy. Each color has its own determinate wavelengths of radiant energy, or light, which the eye distinguishes as being different from one another. As the optic nerve relays these wavelengths to the brain, the brain interprets them as different colors. The longer wavelengths are called *infrared* and the shorter wavelengths are called *ultraviolet*. The longest and shortest waves of light energy are invisible.

Daylight, or white light, is a random mixture of light of all wavelengths. If white light passes through a prism, the random mixture of colors is *sorted.* Its *rainbow,* or *spectrum,* is arranged according to the wavelengths of radiant energy represented. The longest is red, followed by orange, yellow, green, blue, and violet. Wavelengths can be measured in nanometers, which are the equivalent of one-millionth of a millimeter each. The lengths are as follows:

Red	700–650 nanometers
Orange	640–590 nanometers
Yellow	580–550 nanometers
Green	530–490 nanometers
Blue	480–450 nanometers
Violet	440–390 nanometers

This also explains why we perceive different colors throughout the day. As the wavelength of light energy changes, the color we see also changes; however, our brain makes adjustments so we rarely notice variations other than extremes such as sunrises, sunsets, overcast skies, and sunny skies. At dawn or sunset, more of the longer rays—the reddish components—are visible, which create our beautiful sunrises and sunsets. This also means that some colors may look different depending on the time of day we view them. Artificial light sources such as incandescent and fluorescent lighting also have these unbalanced characteristics. Because of these variables, we recommend looking at your color palettes in as many different combinations of light as possible, while trying to replicate the type of light that's going to be in the space on a day-to-day basis. On cloudy days, for example, more of the short, blue-green wavelengths prevail as the longer,

red-orange recede, and the result is that we see bluish grey. Blue or green will appear to be cooler—or more greyish—than when the light source has more of a warm cast to it. If, on the other hand, the colors are warmer, they will appear less warm and more neutral.

When you're selecting colors, you should view color palettes in all forms of light, but most important, in the same type of light that the final colors will be viewed. For example, if you're selecting colors for a room that derives most of its light from natural sources (i.e., sunlight), then pull the color palette together using natural daylight. Also, revisit the palette in the evening with the same types of artificial light that will be used. Considering the artificial light source is important because depending on the part of the world, time of the year, or time of day, supplemental artificial light will be a large contributing factor to the overall color scheme. Different types of artificial light typically have different color renditions. The most popular lamp types are *incandescent, fluorescent,* and *halogen,* which are discussed in more detail in Chapter 3, "Practical Considerations: Selecting Materials and Lighting." When we use the term *lamp,* we're referring primarily to the bulb that lights up, not the type of fixture (table lamp, pendant light, torchère, recessed can, etc.). Incandescent lamps will cast a yellow, warm tone; fluorescent lamps tend toward the blue, cooler tones; and halogen lamps are the most neutral, casting a clearer light that's less likely to distort your color palette. There are also fluorescent lamps on the market now that give warmer colors and full spectrum colors. *Full spectrum* means that the light has all of the colors from the spectrum. Full-spectrum lamps refer to the quality or type of light that's emitted from a lamp. The lamp has been engineered to produce balanced light rays that are also referred to as *white light,* which doesn't affect the value, hue, or intensity of a warm or cool color. This is the most desirable form of light to select, especially if you live in a part of the world with extreme seasonal changes that have short days and long nights during the winter months.

Color Wheels

The basic color wheel starts with three *primary* colors. The three primary colors are *red*, *yellow*, and *blue*. By blending each primary with its adjacent color, we create the *secondary* colors of *orange*, *green*, and *violet*.

Primary Colors

Red, yellow, and blue are the three primary pigment colors. All other colors are derived from various combinations of these three, which are therefore the basis of all color we see (Figure 1.1).

Figure 1.2 *Secondary color wheel.*

Figure 1.1 *Primary color wheel.*

Secondary Colors

When each of the secondary colors shown in Figure 1.2 is placed between the pair of primaries that created it, we have the six-color wheel with the spectrum in its natural order.

Tertiary Colors

Mixing each *primary* and the *adjacent secondary* produces an intermediate *tertiary* color. This results

in the 12-color wheel (Figure 1.3). In an ordered, straight line, we would have colors in their ascending wavelength from blue to yellow to red. When we place the ends together so that they form a circle, we create the color wheel whereby we can combine red with blue to make violet, and so on.

Figure 1.3 *Tertiary color wheel.*

Color Systems

Color systems are technical methods of organizing and ordering color terms into a more universal format. They allow you to create color schemes based on a variety of selection strategies. This is of utmost importance for anyone with color blindness since tertiary colors are less clear and defined than primary and secondary colors. The primary and secondary colors seem pretty straightforward, but once we move into tertiary colors and beyond, color becomes less clear and defined. This is illustrated by terms such as *light, dark, deep, bright,* and *dull.* These are adjectives used to further describe the qualities of colors, but they fall short of truly describing the visual impression of a color. Light and dark tones and shades of beige further complicate the scenario. While these adjectives aren't restricted to tertiary colors and beyond, that's where the terms are frequently applied. By organizing the colors into a pattern, or an ordered color wheel system, you can see the derivation of each and every color and can then select palettes accordingly.

The Munsell Color System

The most widely used color system known is the *Munsell color system.* This system of color designation, developed by Professor Albert H. Munsell (1858–1918), is based on a solid form that is graduated into nine shades of grey. Zero is at the base, which is black, and 10 is at the top, which is white. Grey is the color solid's central axis, and hues are arranged in a wheel around it. The Munsell scale keeps the steps of chroma and value variances constant. *Chroma* is the degree of color intensity, or purity, and is also sometimes referred to as *saturation.* A color that is at its maximum chroma is at its purest and most saturated form. *Value* is a color's lightness or darkness. Because the Munsell system maintains consistent degrees of value and chroma, the solid form of color is an uneven shape. A similar system, developed by Wilhelm Ostwald (1853–1932),

is also based on the color solid. The biggest difference between the Munsell and Ostwald systems is that, in the Ostwald system, varying degrees of color value are applied, which gives a uniform shape to the color solid. (See Figures 1.4 and 1.5.) This geometric shape resembles two identical cones connected at the widest point. Because the Munsell system is the more precise of the two, we'll elaborate on that system in more detail.

In the Munsell system, the colors are first arranged according to their placement in the color spectrum, which is the way we see them in a rainbow. Munsell refers to the color as *hue.* For practical purposes, we'll list the six hues that are represented in the secondary color wheel: red, orange, yellow, green, blue, violet (R, O, Y, G, B, V). The tertiary colors, or hues, between these are then listed as RO, OY, YG, GB, and BV. We can continue to graduate the colors between each hue infinitely, but again, for our purposes here, we'll work with the secondary list of colors as they relate to the spectrum.

Value is the next consideration in the Munsell system. With the six colors arranged in the secondary color wheel, the Munsell system then places graduations of color from light to dark, with white (designated 10 in value) at the top of the scale, black (designated 0 in value) at the bottom of the scale, and nine shades of grey in between. A color's lightness or darkness affects its value but not its hue. The values 1 through 4 are referred to as *shades,* and the values 6 through 9 are referred to as *tints.* In the Munsell system, the value of a color is designated in relation to where the hue sits on the value scale. An example of this would be R/5 (red at value 5), which represents red in its clearest form, at the center of the value scale.

The third aspect of color designation is *chroma.* Chroma is listed in 14 stages, with 1 being minimum and 14 having the maximum, or greatest saturation. A color (hue) with maximum chroma is at its

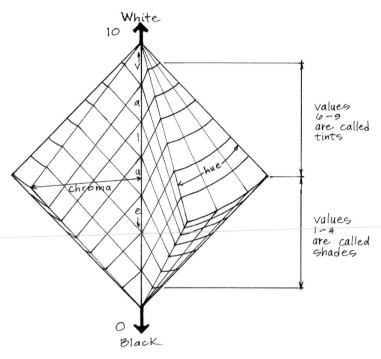

Figure 1.4 Ostwald color system diagram.

purest, clearest form. The minimum chroma is the color in its least saturated form. If we mix the colors at the minimum and maximum ends of the chroma scale, we end up with a neutral grey, which is called *chroma 1*. In the Munsell system, the chroma number designation is last. Our red, value 5, with chroma 7, could then be R/5/7.

Using this system, samples of color can be identified with letter and number codes, which is very helpful for designers working with color selections and is a more precise form of designating each color universally. This color system is the most common one used when working with colors created by dyes and pigments.

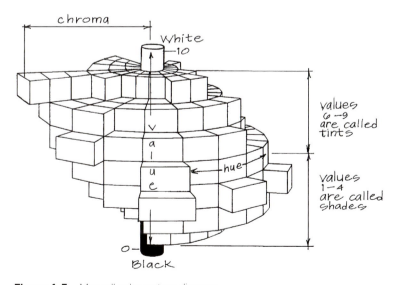

Figure 1.5 Munsell color system diagram.

Additive and Subtractive Color

Colored light, or *additive color,* is produced by passing white light through colored filters, which distorts the color we perceive. Accurate color vision becomes impossible, because everything appears as a tone of the colored light. For example, all colors under a blue light will appear to have a blue cast that doesn't accurately represent the colors illuminated under it. The application of colored light includes stage lighting, lighting displays for clothing, food in supermarkets, and so on. Additive color isn't generally used in interior design because of its tendency to distort color, but it would be used, for example, in a supermarket display to visually alter fresh food on display. The greens in the vegetable display would appear greener (therefore fresher), or the meat might have red tints added in the lighting so that it appears more red. This is not necessarily a deceptive practice, since color may actually be distorted by artificial store lighting, and the additive lighting then is used to adjust rather than to alter. The color mixtures of additive color are obtained by adding the wavelengths that represent the three primary colors (red, blue, and yellow), so if green is to be enhanced, more blue and yellow might be used, depending on the amount of adjustment desired.

Subtractive color is the most widely used form of color. (See Figure 1.6.) Any time we paint, print, or dye an object or material, we're working with subtractive color. Subtractive color means the object or material absorbs—or subtracts—all the colors *except* the color of the object. A red object absorbs all colors except red and reflects back only red light.

Warm and Cool Colors

If we were to draw a line through the center of the color wheel with red, orange, and yellow on one side and green, blue, and violet on the other, each side would have a very different feel that we could describe as warm or cool. The warm colors are the red, orange, yellow varieties, and the cool colors are the green, blue, violet varieties. These associations with temperatures stem from color descriptions such as "red hot," "warm yellow sun," "cool blue ice," "cool blue-green water," "warm orange sunsets," and so on. The color and temperature associations are not scientifically accurate, but they nevertheless persist because, to most people, colors just seem to be warm or cool. For example, the blue at the center of a flame has a higher temperature than the orange and yellow portions, yet we believe blue to be a cool color. As we know, the shorter wavelength at the blue-violet end of the color spectrum is of a higher frequency and therefore has the greatest capacity to generate heat, whereas the longer wavelengths at the red end of the spectrum generate the least amount of heat. Still, people will likely continue to think of red as warm and violet as cool.

In practical application, using colors from the warm side of the color wheel allows us to create a space that's visually warm and cozy. Using colors from the warm side of the color wheel can be especially useful in a space where natural light may be unavailable. The warm feel of the sun cannot be replaced by artificial light alone, but add warm, bright sunny tones, and the absence of natural light is far less noticeable. Geographical influences are also important. Let's say you live in a very warm climate and you want to create a cool, quiet atmosphere. By using colors from the cool side of the color wheel, you can be successful in visually cooling the space.

Color Palettes

At this point, you should have an understanding of the basics of color. What follows are some guidelines on color combinations. As you can imagine, the possibilities are endless; however, the illustra-

Figure 1.6 In this apartment entry, the color palette consists of contrasting hues that are all in the same, neutral color family. In addition to the spectacular use of natural materials and symmetry, the extreme contrast adds much visual interest. *(Arq. Diego Matthai, IIDA, Matthai Arquitectos.)*

tions and text in the following sections are a good starting point for color selection. (See Figures 1.7 and 1.8.)

Light Shades

The lightness or darkness of a color is called its *value* and is dependent on the amount of light it absorbs or reflects. Figures 1.9 through 1.13 illus-

trate the subtle impact that color value and the use of light shades in color palettes can have.

Primary Color Palettes

Red, yellow, and blue are the three primary pigment colors. All other colors are derived from various combinations of these three; therefore, they're the basis of all color we see. (See Figures 1.14 to 1.19.)

Figure 1.7 In this photo the red used accentuates the artwork, which has a black-and-white theatrical quality. *(Tom Gass, IIDA, Gass Design. Photo by Peter Paige.)*

Figure 1.8 Using dark colors with wood tones creates a cozy backdrop for the contrasting reading chair and pillow. *(Treena Crochet, A Matter of Style, Ltd. Photo © Stephen SetteDucati.)*

Figure 1.9A and 1.9B The rich wood tones are enhanced by the light hues of the wall and wainscot. The accessories bring warmth and elegance to the room. *(Maria P. Perron, Village House Interiors, LLC. Mike Rixon Photography, Bow, New Hampshire.)*

Figure 1.10 As with color value, the relative lightness and darkness is dependent on the amount of water flowing over this terraced rock bed. *(Russ Dillingham.)*

Figure 1.11 The wood flooring, rattan furnishings, and area rug in this bedroom add warmth to the light, neutral tones of the walls and bedding. *(Lori W. Carroll, ASID, IIDA. William Lesch Photography.)*

Figure 1.12 Creative lighting enhances the sage green walls and white architectural elements in this room. *(Douglas Kahn/Gould Evans.)*

Figure 1.13 The dusty pink tint of this open space creates a soothing haven for guests. The inviting lush green yard becomes an extension of the interior. *(Arq. Diego Matthai, IIDA, Matthai Arquitectos. Photo by Sebastian Saldivar.)*

Figure 1.14 We often see dramatic sunsets with red, yellow, and blue, but forget that it is nature's representation of primary color. When selecting color palettes for our homes, the tendency is to be subtle and oftentimes timid with the use of color strong in value and chroma; however, if we look to nature for guidance, we see some of the most vivid and clear examples of its potential. *(Russ Dillingham.)*

Figure 1.15 The ultimate balance is created by using the three primary colors. Typically, when we think of primary color palettes, we visualize bright, solid red, yellow, and blue crayonlike colors. This dining area is a marvelous example of using primary colors to create a soft, restful space. *(Arq. Diego Matthai, IIDA, Matthai Arquitectos. Photo by Sebastian Saldivar.)*

Figures 1.16 and 1.17 This is a more subdued example of the use of primary colors that allows the artwork and architectural detail to carry the design statement. *(Gill Smith, Interior and Landscape Designer, Aukland, New Zealand.)*

Figure 1.18 The deep blue walls are well balanced by the use of contrasting colors in the artwork, making this space very dynamic. Again, primary colors have been used. *(K2S Design Studio; Kathryn B. Adams and Stephanie Skovron.)*

Figure 1.19 The bright cheerfulness of this artwork demonstrates the dynamic impact that primary colors have on an interior space. *(Photo by Peter Paige.)*

Monochromatic and Monotone Palettes

When creating a monochromatic palette, the object is to layer colors that are in the same family or adjacent to one another on the color wheel. Monochromatic palettes use only one hue or value of any color in varying shades and tints. Monotone palettes differ from monochromatic palettes in that they use only neutral colors such as beige or grey, but various shades, hues, and values. (See Figures 1.20 to 1.23.) If you're working with primarily light or medium tones, you may want to accent with a color of darker saturation. If you're timid about using too much strong or dark color with a monochromatic palette, start by selecting one area in each room to use as a focal point, and use the strongest color value there. This will enable you to keep the intensity with the rest of the room less bold. Monochromatic palettes also have a simpler, more elegant appearance, will help avoid a cluttered look, and are especially good to use when the space is small. The uniformity in color will visually quiet the space and can make it appear larger.

If the color palette in a space is all from the same color family, then the eye doesn't perceive many details such as window and door openings, built-in

Figure 1.20 As this sunset reminds us, monochromatic color palettes don't have to be neutral colors. *(Russ Dillingham.)*

Figure 1.21 In this bedroom, the soft monotone palette allows the boldness of the framed mirror to stand alone, and the room's occupant becomes the focal point. *(Gauthier-Stacy, Inc. Photo by Sam Gray.)*

bookcases, and so on. When the space is small, there tends to be less wall area between the doors and windows. The visual trick of a monocolor palette is very helpful when the space has many exposed details from plumbing, wiring, structural framing, or air-conditioning systems. The same trick can be applied when selecting colors for walls and trim. Try to visualize the window and/or door opening with a light color, then with a dark color.

The darker the color on the trim, the more it will look like the opening has been outlined, as with a crayon or marker. If the trim color is finished in a color the same as or lighter than the wall, it will appear to blend into the wall, and the overall effect will be one of the whole wall appearing larger because it is not visually broken up by the interruption of the opening.

Figures 1.22 and 1.23 This contemporary bedroom suite highlights the architectural details of the space and provides a calming, quiet retreat. *(Michael Spillers/Gould Evans.) (Douglas Kahn/Gould Evans.)*

Contrasting Palettes

Contrasting color palettes occur when complementary colors in various tones, hues, and chromas are used together within the same space, often against a neutral background. (See Figures 1.24 to 1.28.) When these complementary colors are combined in this way, they are considered to be at their maximum intensities. In other words, using light and dark hues at extreme ends of contrast will make a

Figure 1.24 This photo of the multitoned sunflower wouldn't be as dramatic if it weren't cast against a brilliant blue sky. *(Russ Dillingham.)*

Figure 1.25 The almost stark neutral tones in this apartment give the boldness in the artwork and accessories a gallery-like setting. The drama is further enhanced with the striking texture of the iron handrails and the fireplace surround. *(Gayle Reynolds, ASID, IIDA. Steve Vierra Photography.)*

Figure 1.26 This photo illustrates how colors can be layered to create a contrasting palette. Here, the dark wood finish, a red fireplace surround, and the coordinating sofa and cushions complete the scheme. The walls have been finished in a light tone, allowing the fireplace and furnishings to create the contrasts. *(Gill Smith, Interior and Landscape Designer, Aukland, New Zealand.)*

Figure 1.27 The striking contrast of the faux painted green walls against the white trim and shutters, give this dining room a southern appeal. The period furnishings and the hardwood flooring contribute to the warmth and charm of the space. *(Photo by Peter Paige.)*

Figure 1.28 *Extreme contrasts, such as these linens and artwork against the walls, can have an impact opposite from what is expected. This room has a soothing and calming appeal even though contrasts are used.* (Photo by Peter Paige.)

bold statement with strong visual impact. The key to remember with contrasting palettes is balance. When too much of one color is displayed, the resulting space can feel unbalanced or too flat. The addition of its complement effectively balances it. If you have a dominant yellow theme, look for accessories and details in bright blue to balance the palette.

Complementary Palettes

A complementary color palette is achieved when colors directly opposite from each other on the color wheel are used together. Examples of complementary palettes are green with red, orange with blue, and yellow with violet. Complementary palettes are most successful when lower levels of chroma (color intensity) for the hues are used. It is also acceptable to include an adjacent color on the wheel, such as red with green-blue or green-yellow. (See Figures 1.29 and 1.30.)

Figure 1.29 *Blue sky complements the orange-yellow in the leaves.* (Russ Dillingham.)

Figure 1.30 The use of complementary palettes can be subtle, as shown in this Southwestern dining space. All of the complementary colors used in the area rug and upholstery have been punctuated with a higher intensity in the plant and painting. It is also worth noting that the painting has added visual impact by being unframed, which gives it an unconfined look rather than limiting its place on the wall. *(Lori W. Carroll, ASID, IIDA. William Lesch Photography.)*

Color Saturation and Intensity

Color saturation, or chroma, is the component that we perceive as the relative brightness or dullness of the color. A color's saturation or intensity is at its maximum when used with its complement. In other words, to increase the impact of a particular palette, use its complementary color (the color on the opposite side of the color wheel) in accent objects and materials. Yellow-orange when accented with blue-violet, red with green, and blue with orange, all become more intense or saturated when used together. (See Figures 1.31 to 1.35.)

Figure 1.31 *The color palette of red and yellow and the complementary color of the pollen-collecting insect have combined to create maximum color saturation and intensity. (Russ Dillingham.)*

Figure 1.32 *The highly saturated wall color in this living room is maximized by the deep complementary colors in the artwork and marble fireplace surround. (Gill Smith, Interior and Landscape Designer, Aukland, New Zealand.)*

Figure 1.33   Color saturation can be done without becoming overwhelming when one element or accent balances with lightness. In this room, the two significant paintings are very light tones. *(Andrew Liberty Interiors, IIDA.)*

Figure 1.34 The use of traditional colonial colors such as golden yellow, dusty blues, or mossy greens, to name a few, are best suited to spaces with strong traditional architectural details, as in this sitting area. *(Photograph and design by Susan Stowell for Interior Solutions.)*

Figure 1.35 The rich gold paint of this room and the primary colors of the artwork and furniture illustrate the drama of color saturation and intensity on a space. *(Photo by Peter Paige.)*

Natural Color Palettes

Whatever period, region, or style your living space is, finding the perfect palette of colors may be as simple as looking beyond the front door. Natural and regional palettes can be achieved with paint, plants, artwork, and natural materials.

If you want your home to have a Southwestern feel, chili pepper reds, rich gold, and cacti greens are appropriate. If the space is in a coastal region, soft seashell tones, bright sea glass accents, silvery greys, and evergreens will work. Of course, there's no reason to limit your color palettes to those commonly associated with the area you live in, and if those palettes don't fit your own style preference, then explore one that does, and use it to create your own personalized space. (See Figures 1.36 to 1.40.)

Figure 1.36 *Natural light helps to enhance the natural color palette of this room. Here, simple monochromatic tones, natural wood, and warm clay accents make the room rich and inviting. The rustic finish of the coffee table and the organic lines in the wood side chairs further enhance the simplicity of the space. (Gayle Reynolds, ASID, IIDA. Photo © Eric Roth.)*

Figure 1.37   The use of wood with the green and muted-white palette shows how natural color palettes can create a peaceful setting for a room. *(Gayle Reynolds, ASID, IIDA. Steve Vierra Photography.)*

Figure 1.38 This striking transition area becomes a natural extension of the outdoor environment by maintaining wood finishes in many forms, highlighting the stonework with light and the use of an organic floor finish. *(Christina Oliver Interiors. Brian Vanden Brink, Photographer © 2002.)*

Figure 1.39 Whereas the space shown in Figure 1.36 becomes a natural extension of its surroundings, this space showcases the use of color, texture, and form to demonstrate that natural color palettes are not always derived from organic sources. The walls, in subtle green and brown hues, have many interesting textures and forms that deliver a natural feel. The accent lighting and sculpture give the additional depth and texture often associated with organic design. *(Michael Spillars/Gould Evans.)*

Figure 1.40 This organic setting is rich with texture and variety of materials, yet maintains a neutral, organic feel. *(Russ Dillingham.)*

Integrating Natural Materials with Color Palettes

Color palettes can be enhanced by using natural materials within the living space (assuming that natural materials are integral to the look you're trying to achieve). Some designers believe that including natural materials allows us to feel more connected with nature. Whether you believe this or not, it does make sense to incorporate something organic into your color palette. If this is your choice, each room should include one or more forms of natural materials. For example, a kitchen can have wood cabinets with marble or granite countertops.

A more organic approach to using natural materials is to think of them as they appear in their natural habitat, and the first place to focus is to the floor. While a dirt floor isn't a likely choice, wood, cork, stone, tile, and natural woven carpets in organic colors and tones are appropriate. Think of the floor as the foundation for the rest of your finish selections. Color palettes can include browns, greys, beiges, moss tones, burgundies, and patterns that have organic shapes and lines. You may choose a wood or stone floor with area rugs to add color and visual contrast. Plants are the most obvious way to bring nature inside for any particular room, and they create a great transitional element for leading the eye from the floor up toward the walls and ceiling. Floor plants need a container that will blend nicely with the floor, creating an accent of color or texture. If you want to use several natural materials within a living space, you can add color with the wall finishes, window treatments, artwork, and accessories. Be mindful of the lighting choices selected—make sure they don't contradict the effect you're trying to achieve. For example, a room that incorporates many natural elements is not the place to use fluorescent lamps or to rely too much on direct light sources. Indirect and ambient sources with halogen and incandescent lamps are good choices. You may also want to try some accent lighting and backlighting for added drama. Remember, natural light can be very dramatic! (See Figures 1.41 to 1.44.)

Figure 1.41 *The wood cabinets and granite countertops in this kitchen are subtle, allowing the food served to provide accent color. The light walls along with the natural wood floors and furniture are another way to integrate natural materials with this kitchen's simple color palette. (Gayle Reynolds, ASID, IIDA. Steve Vierra Photography.)*

Figure 1.42 This shower enclosure displays the exclusive use of natural materials on all surfaces and is further enhanced by the addition of simple greenery. This adds to the softness and texture often lacking in an environment created exclusively with natural materials. *(Lori W. Carroll, ASID, IIDA. William Lesch Photography.)*

Figure 1.43 The textural variety within this dining room adds interest where color is used in a subtle way. The bamboo ceiling adds a textural element that contributes a sense of scale and proportion by being slightly lower than the rest of the space. *(Lori W. Carroll, ASID, IIDA. William Lesch Photography.)*

Figure 1.44 In addition to the natural color tones used in this bathroom, the designer has also implemented the use of several organic materials such as natural bamboo, tiles on the walls and counters, and a natural-finish mirror frame. It is a good example of how accessorizing can complete a look. *(Lori W. Carroll, ASID, IIDA. William Lesch Photography.)*

Getting Started with a Color Palette

Trying to decide how to get started with your color scheme? If you have a decorative rug or carpet, working with its accent colors may help you get under way. Accessories and artwork are other excellent choices to help you launch your color initiatives for that small space design. Existing pieces of furniture and accent pillows may also be desirable areas to focus on at the beginning of your selections for the interior. Remember to follow your instincts—examine your wardrobe for cues to the colors you're naturally drawn to, or perhaps make use of an image from a magazine that caught your attention. Explore. Have fun with the process. The key to a successful space is in what makes you feel comfortable and happy. (See Figures 1.45 to 1.48.)

Summary

The principles of color explain what it is. Understanding the principles allows us to use color well, with a sense of process and order. We can look to the color wheels and charts and see a color's complement, contrast, or coordinating color options. Understanding those principles makes the process easy. The part that's not so easy to explain is why we're drawn to some colors but not others, or how some colors relate to psychology and physiology, proportion, natural and artificial light sources, and so on. Now that we've outlined the fundamentals of color and explored the various standard color palette combinations, we'll shift our focus to exploring these other color relationships.

Figure 1.45 *Enjoy your collectibles and personalize your rooms when you display them. Integrating one or more colors from a favorite piece will add distinction to your color scheme. (Photo by Peter Paige.)*

Figure 1.46 *The fine collectibles displayed in this room are an example of using special pieces for a look that personalizes your space. (Photo by Peter Paige.)*

Figure 1.47 The soft pastels of this bedroom are balanced and enhanced by the use of bold artwork and the rich colors in the draperies and floral arrangement. This striking balance creates a restful space. *(Photo by Peter Paige.)*

Figure 1.48 In some apartment settings, painting the walls is not always an option. When this is the case, color can be added to the space with furniture and accessories. Your own collectibles can easily personalize any space. *(Gill Smith, Interior and Landscape Designer, Aukland, New Zealand.)*

CHAPTER 2
Color and Proportion

One of the various ways in which color can visually enhance, embellish, and modify a room's overall appearance is through our use of color and its proportion in the space. This is particularly useful when dealing with a space that is overly large, very small, or unusual in shape. We also need to have insight into the varying psychological and physiological responses so that we can use the colors with appropriate proportion and placement.

In this chapter we'll extend our understanding of color to include the less defined parameters that relate to our senses. We'll discuss the following:

- Color and proportion

- Physiological responses

- Psychological implications

- Specific color associations

- How light affects color

- Color and dimension

- Zoning with color

- The use of mirrors, accessories, and plants to define space

Manipulating the Size of a Space with Color

Since color can alter the scale and proportion of a room, there are many considerations to color application when we have a space that's either too big or small. Here are a few principles to guide your wall color selection process when proportion isn't ideal.

- *Pattern.* Small-scale patterns will look like a solid color from a distance, whereas larger, less intricate patterns read more as separate colors. Smaller patterns also give the perception of more volume, whereas larger-scale patterns can have the opposite effect. If your intent is to create the illusion of more space, stay away from patterns that are too bold and large. Another aspect of patterns to note is the repeat of the pattern. If the pattern repeat is very regular and even, it will be difficult to look at in a large amount of it, and can appear to vibrate if you look at it too long. Most of us have experienced this type of optical illusion, which occurs when the eye tries to focus on too many copies of the same shape at once. Select patterns that have a random repeat and less contrast among the colors in the pattern.

- *Finish and texture.* If the finish of a surface is smooth and glossy, the color will appear to be more diluted than what was intended. Heavily textured surfaces will visually darken colors due to shadowing and lack of reflectiveness (less light reflects off of it). A metallic finish will also appear lighter, but will have an undertone of whatever metal is being portrayed, thus muting the intended color. Silver or pewter metals will add a cool tone to the color, whereas gold, copper, or bronze will contribute warmth to the color. If the metal has a mirrorlike finish, it will reflect whatever color is around it. Experiment with and adjust the intensity or darkness of the intended color to get it right.

- *Adjacent colors.* These can alter the appearance (value and hue) of a color. If you're using light colors and the adjacent areas are a dark color, the light colors will appear lighter than they really are and the dark colors will appear darker by contrast. Light-colored objects also appear to weigh less than the same-size object of a dark color. Cool colors appear to recede, or to look farther away than they actually are, while warm colors seem to come closer. Let's say, for example, you have an awkwardly shaped room that has an overly small wall next to an overly large or long room (by proportion): By applying a very light or luminescent color to the smallish wall and a deeper contrasting color on the larger wall, you can visually balance the room's proportion somewhat. You can then finish the effect with artwork. A large, bold, light-colored print added to the darker wall will further emphasize the lighter wall and balance the space nicely.

By understanding these simple principles, you can manipulate a space with color placement. If the space is busy, or has many angles, corners, doors, windows, recesses, and soffits, one neutral color for the walls and trim will give a cleaner, less cluttered appearance. This is a common issue with small spaces, because we have less wall and floor area, but perhaps as many doors and windows as a larger space.

Neutral color for the walls and trim will create a cleaner, less cluttered appearance. You can use a higher-gloss paint finish on the trim than on the walls, but stick with one color—or at least stay within a shade or two of the same color. This is not a hard-and-fast rule, because there are many levels of busyness and complexity with different spaces, but it's a good rule of thumb.

You can use color to add drama, create a focal point, or highlight an object or area of the room. Introducing strong-hued color to a neutral color palette is an easy way to create a focal point, whether it's in an accent color for a wall, rug, or piece of furniture. If you have a long and narrow or asymmetrical room, try applying warmer, darker shades on the shorter walls and lighter colors on the longer ones to help balance the proportions. This principle is often applied to ceilings, since a white ceiling seems higher and more open than a dark ceiling. Conversely, when the ceiling is very high and the resulting space lacks warmth or intimacy, paint it in darker, warmer tones. Texture is another good way to add visual depth and drama to the ceiling with materials such as textured tin panels, which will enhance any color with the shade and shadow inherent in the profile.

The Psychology and Physiology of Color

The psychological impact of color is widely recognized and accepted. It has been shown to alter moods, emotions, physical responses, and our overall perception of the spaces around us. People have been known to feel differently in the presence of varying colors, both in what they wear and in their environments. This has been a useful tool for psychotherapists to use in their understanding of a person's psyche. Spaces with cool temperatures can be painted, accessorized, and lighted anew with warm colors, tones, and light fixtures, and the occupants of the space would perceive that the space was physically warmer, even in the absence of any actual temperature change.

Color is the element of design that has more physiological impact than any other. It has the ability to relax and soothe us, to stimulate our senses, or just to make us feel better. Studies have even determined which colors are most appropriate for different applications. In Faber Birren's book, *Color and Human Response,* he refers to the studies on the emotional effects of color conducted by Felix Deutsch in 1937. Birren concludes that light energy directly affects the body through the eye and brain. Deutsch also found that emotional reactions to color are based on our personal and historical memory associations with that color. Some of these associations are as follows:

COLOR	ASSOCIATIONS
Yellow	The sun, the sun's warmth, cheerfulness
Blue	The sky, the ocean, coolness, tranquility
Red	Life, rebirth, heat, fire, strength, and power
Green	Forests, meadows, healing, rest, renewal, tranquility
Purple	Royalty, spiritual matters, healing, magic
Orange	Oranges, energy, connected to yellow and red, known to stimulate the appetite
Brown	The earth, wood, natural surroundings, neutral

These associations can establish particular attitudes toward colors. Modifying an interior environment can enhance your sense of well-being and outlook on life through your emotions and mental processes. The following sections describe some widely accepted color associations in detail.

Psychological Color Associations

Red is seen as warm, exciting, stimulating, and even aggressive. Historically, it's been associated with blood, fire, evil, vitality, power, and strength. It's a difficult color to use in large quantities because of these associations, but it can be quite effective if used with discretion. As an accent color, it carries a lot of impact.

Orange has attributes similar to red, but to a lesser degree. It's linked to both red and yellow. When used with red, it softens red's intensity, whereas when used with yellow, it has the ability to warm and energize. It has been shown to affect the autonomic nervous system to stimulate the appetite, which explains why so much of it is used in the food-packaging industry. Because it's less intense than red, we can use a larger quantity of it in our color schemes. In higher intensities, it works best as an accent, but in lower intensities, it has a much broader appeal.

Yellow, at the warm end of the spectrum, is the most widely used color in interior design. It's associated with sunny dispositions and cheerfulness. Because of its brightness, it's a great choice for visually warming a space that's harsh or cold. Unlike other colors, yellow can be used freely in various tints and hues. Try using several hues of yellow in rooms that get little to no natural light, and the room will feel sunnier and brighter. (See Figure 2.1.)

Greens are the cool colors closest to the warm end of the color spectrum. They're widely used for color palettes that are restful, restorative, relaxing, and peaceful due to their association with nature and restful places such as meadows and mountainsides. Because of this association, it's no wonder that greens are also widely used in school and hospital interiors. An unfortunate fallout of its application in such spaces, however, was that the greens often chosen for these interiors contained grey or muddy tones (hence, "institutional green"). Scientifically, consider the phenomenon known as *afterimage,* which occurs when we focus on one color for a long period of time, look away, and "see" the color that is directly opposite on the color wheel. When this phenomenon was discovered, it reinforced the notion that operating rooms should be painted green, because when a surgeon is focused on the bright color red during long operations and then looks away, she or he will see green spots. This can be very fatiguing to the optic nerve. By painting the walls green, eye fatigue can be reduced.

Figure 2.1   *Just imagine what Mother Nature was thinking when palettes of red, orange, violet, blue, and green were combined and then softly accented with silver fern. (Russ Dillingham.)*

Blue is the quintessential cool color. People think of it as being restful, calming, and quiet. If overused or used in strong chroma, it can be depressing or gloomy. High intensities of blue can be effectively used as accents to balance warm palettes. (See Figure 2.2.)

Violet is a very complex color. It's achieved by mixing red, the warmest color on the spectrum, with blue, the coolest color on the spectrum. Highly creative people are often drawn to purple and violet. Violet has the highest frequency in the visible spectrum, which is why many New Age believers see violet as the color connected to spiritual intuition and why it has been used for centuries in churches, temples, and places of worship.

Figure 2.2 Hues of blue-violet, as with the berries shown here, work equally well with contrasting or complementary palettes. *(Russ Dillingham.)*

Neutrals include light to medium browns. Neutrals are known by names such as *buff, beige, nude, bisque, ecru,* and *cream.* They are subtle, unpretentious, and classic colors. The very name *neutral* evokes natural. Natural colors, with names such as *golden straw, desert dust, lamb's wool,* and *cornhusk,* are the lightest of the earth tones. These were popularized in the 1920s by the Bauhaus School of Architecture and Art, whose principles were those of simplicity and organic design. Today, virtually any color found in nature, when used in its palest hue, can be considered neutral. (See Figure 2.3.)

White evokes a sense of purity, simplicity, and innocence. It's the color of beginnings, of newness. We're christened in white, married in white (interestingly, however, white is used for mourning in Asia). The purest white contains all the colors of the spectrum. The human eye sees white as brilliant color, so too much pure white causes eyestrain and can exacerbate the condition of afterimage. While white can be a great background color, too much white can become monotonous. If you're considering all-white walls, it would be better to select an off-white or a warm white.

Black can be sleek, sophisticated, and dramatic or sinister, eerie, and dark. It's a formal color—the little black dress, black-tie formal—and it's the color associated with mourning and death. As a color in our living spaces, too much black can create a cavelike feel. Black works best for accessories, case goods, and upholstered furnishings. Because it absorbs light, black is a difficult color to use on a large area such as a wall, but can be used effectively on floors with material like marble or slate tiles, in textured or patterned carpets, and for bed linens, window treatments, laminates, counters, and so on. Paired with white, it creates the quintessential contrast, which can be classic, eclectic, savvy, and dramatic. (See Figure 2.4.)

Figure 2.3 Warm neutral tones are naturally balanced against the cool blue of the water and sky. *(Russ Dillingham.)*

Figure 2.4 The elusive loon quietly displays its intricate, dramatic black-and-white colors against the mossy green water. Since the color of a space has both psychological and physiological effects on people, it's important to take these associations into account when selecting a color scheme. *(Russ Dillingham.)*

Color and Light

The size and shape of a room, the sources of light, and the function of the room should all be considered when choosing a color palette. We briefly discussed the principles of color and light in Chapter 1, and we are now ready to discuss lighting applications in more detail.

One of the more intangible elements of good design is lighting. Creating ambience in a room, especially in the evening, can be accomplished with the correct use of light. When considering general illumination for an environment, the goal is to provide light that produces a warm glow, enhances the colors of the finishes and furnishings, and flatters the skin tones of your guests, known as *color rendition*. Color rendition is important to keep in mind when you want to create a space that flatters its occupants.

Lighting can be nondescript or can be treated as a decorative element, as with a lamp, torchère, or pendant light. Providing light for work, reading, or playing board games can be accomplished with *task lighting* (i.e., providing additional light for specific activities). Task lighting can be achieved with table lamps or with recessed or track lights that have been wired with dimmer switching to allow for various levels of light.

Lighting is an important consideration when selecting interior finish colors. If the environment is in a cooler climate, you may want to use more incandescent fixtures, since they tend to cast a yellow, warm tone of light. If your goal is to warm a space, you may also want to use colors from the warm side of the color wheel to dominate the color scheme, and you want to avoid hues of beige and drab tones in your palettes. If you want to use a neutral palette, choose the warm whites and then accent with stronger additive colors. In a warmer environment, the opposite tactic would be appro-

priate. While incandescent fixtures would not necessarily be a no-no, it would be best to use them in applications where they can reflect off of a cool-toned surface instead of for lamps and direct light sources. For more information on lighting, see Chapter 3.

Daylight

Daylight is the most preferred form of light for illuminating a living space. Manufacturers of artificial light sources try to duplicate the effect of natural light. This is because sunlight contains all of the colors in the spectrum. When all of these colors are present, the light that is created is vibrant, white, and does not distort our perception of the colors surrounding us. Physiologically, it affects us in the following ways:

- On the glandular level, the pineal and pituitary glands located behind our eyes are affected. Both glands are light-sensitive and are responsible for regulating our hormones.

- These hormones help to

    Regulate our body clocks

    Form melanin (pigment) in our skin

    Improve our ability to see

    Boost our brain's ability to function efficiently

    Increase our body's ability to synthesize vitamins

As researchers continue to explore the effects of full- or natural-spectrum light, they are uncovering some of its health benefits:

- Enhances release of the hormone seratonin

- Reduces neurosis such as panic attacks, insomnia, and headaches

- Enhances vitamin D production

- Lowers blood pressure and LDL cholesterol

- Lessens seasonal affective disorder (SAD)

- Reduces hyperactivity

- Reduces eyestrain

- Increases color rendition, which enhances visual acuity

- Reduces melatonin levels (a hormone that promotes fatigue)

- Stimulates circulation

- Enhances white blood cell production, which boosts the immune function

Typical artificial light sources have the following color-rendition problems:

- Incandescent bulbs emphasize the orange-to-red end of the spectrum. This compromises the quality of the blue and violet colors.

- Fluorescent bulbs overemphasize the yellow-to-green parts of the spectrum. The yellow-to-green colors become so dominant that all other colors of the spectrum are distorted (including the yellow and green colors).

With this much distortion, it is easy to understand why these sources of light are poor choices from both quality-of-color and health perspectives. Natural-spectrum lightbulbs have been developed to replicate daylight as closely as possible. Some manufacturers do this by coating the surface of the bulbs with materials that balance the light they emit. Incandescent bulbs use a layer of an element called *neodymium,* and fluorescent bulbs use a blend of phosphors. To balance the wavelengths, they reduce the ability of undesirable dominant colors to pass through the bulb surface, accentuate certain colors, and add or create new ones, including ultraviolet (UV) wavelengths. The resulting light is as close to full-spectrum light as possible, with many colors represented at once.

Geographically, the best quality of full-spectrum light (daylight) exists at 12:00 P.M. at the equator. While we can't all live at the equator, we should make every effort to obtain the best quality of full-spectrum light available in all of our artificial sources whenever we need to supplement daylight.

While lighting manufacturers have created many interesting fixtures and lamp types, the key element for re-creating the look of natural light is to consider how natural light comes into a space. If you look at natural light, it has shade, a shadow, and areas that are brighter than others. Achieving the look of natural light requires that you place your light sources so that they reflect off of objects. In other words, light the walls and objects in a space rather than lighting only the space. (See Figures 2.5 and 2.6.)

Evening Light

Evening light can be soft and glowing or very dramatic, depending on the use of the space. When designing a space, many architects and designers consider the effect of interior forms, exterior windows, and, of course, the type of light sources to be used. Unless it's a workspace, you don't need to be concerned with trying to re-create daytime. If the space is used for socializing, the light levels don't need to be very high. Try directing most of the light sources toward a wall or object to create shade, shadow, or texture. If the walls are painted in warm colors, the warmth of the light will be enhanced. If the walls are painted cool colors, the colors will still be enhanced, but will also tend to brighten the space. Either way, indirect light sources (light that's reflected off of a ceiling, wall, or object) will be more soothing. If the space includes an area that will be used for reading or playing games, add task lighting, which will also add visual interest to these areas.

Evening Light for the Kitchen

Evening light for the kitchen is also important to consider, since most kitchen tasks require a well-lit environment. Food-preparation areas need to be very well lit, while the general circulation areas can have softer lighting. We like to light kitchens using a *three-point principle.* The first point is to provide

Figure 2.6 *This entry area uses neutral colors to effectively reflect the natural daylight from multiple sources within the space. The floral arrangement contributes a splash of color and becomes a focal point. (Chris Jordan, Designcorp.)*

Figure 2.5 *This palette of leaves would look very flat and plain if it were not for the reflected light from the water and the subtle shading. (Russ Dillingham.)*

good overall light for general circulation. Recessed halogen lights are good options for overall lighting; if possible, position them 12 inches to center from the face of your wall cabinets and 2 to 3 feet apart. This positioning allows the light to shine on the counter in front of you instead of from behind you, which would create a shadow on the counter. The second point of the three-point principle of lighting for the kitchen is to place a light source under cabinets. This is an effective way to light the whole countertop and often serves as the softest overall illumination. The third point is, of course, task lighting, which can be achieved with one or more low-voltage lights that illuminate a specific surface area very brightly. Task lighting is also known for its lack of glare in the eye zone and is a great solution for illumination of any surface area where you want to avoid the visual obstruction of a pendant or track light. Another form

Figure 2.7 In natural environments, sunsets became more dramatic as they create contrast, shadow, and textural silhouettes. *(Russ Dillingham.)*

of task lighting is a decorative pendant, which can add a wonderful visual accent and is a good way to personalize any space. All of these forms of light can be made even more flexible with the addition of dimming switches. (See Figures 2.7 and 2.8.)

Evening Light for the Bathroom

The bathroom is another room that requires attention to detail when selecting light sources. A bathroom is typically lit with either one fan/light combination unit and/or a vanity light. While this approach to lighting isn't wrong, it's definitely uninspired. If this is the bathroom lighting situation

Figure 2.8 The neutral tones of this living and dining space have been richly enhanced by the warm tones that literally glow in the evening with the help from the indirect dining-room light fixture and the fireplace. *(Braun Design, Ltd., Maura Braun, IIDA. Photo © George Lambrose, Lambrose Photography, Inc.)*

you're faced with and you can't change it, try removing the bulb from the fan/light fixture and adding either a lamp, a beautiful torchère, or a pendant light for general lighting needs.

If you're able to choose your own bathroom lighting, consider similar principles to those we discussed for the kitchen. In other words, you'll need good general light (it doesn't need to be bright), uniform task light for shaving and applying makeup, and if possible a bit of accent light. Because of the limited size of most bathrooms, a lighting technique known as *wall grazing* can be used effectively. Wall grazing is done by installing either recessed fixtures

or track lighting no more than 12 inches from the wall and spaced 12 to 24 inches apart depending on the size of the room. This technique provides dramatic light that will reveal any texture on the wall (such as brick, tile, or stone). It will also light polished surfaces such as marble or mirrors without distracting reflections. (See Figures 2.9 to 2.12.)

Be sure to check your local codes when changing kitchen or bathroom lighting because many require bulbs or switches to be a particular distance away from water sources.

Figure 2.9 The indirect light source in this bedroom in combination with the rich, warm tones in the artwork on display create a cozy environment for relaxing. Note that the base palette is monotone, but the accents use the three primary colors, which create a very dramatic effect. *(Chris Jordan, Designcorp.)*

Figures 2.10 and 2.11 The opulence of this dining-room seating is balanced by the soft seating behind it. The backdrop of the cityscape creates a sense of sparkle and grandeur. *(Gauthier-Stacy, Inc. Photographer: Sam Gray.)*

Figure 2.12 The rich tropical color palette of this space takes on a jewel-like quality with evening light in this lush paradise. *(Arq. Diego Matthai, IIDA, Matthai Arquitectos. Photo by Sebastian Saldivar.)*

Seasonal Light

Seasonal light is, as its name implies, the type of light available throughout the seasonal cycles of the year. Much is known and has been written on how we are affected by the light and, more important, how we are affected by the lack of it, resulting in conditions such as *seasonal affected disorder* (SAD). However, we're not going to discuss the physiological aspects here. Instead, we want to focus on color and, more specifically, how seasonal light drives us to use particular colors.

Looking at the contrasts between the Northern and Southern Hemispheres of our planet, it's interesting to note the different color palettes that are commonly used in each region. In climates where winter lasts longer, brighter, bolder colors are often used in an attempt to warm and brighten landscapes and interior spaces. Bright reds and yellows are often used in regions where a wintry climate dominates. In contrast, the warmer climates favor lighter and cooler tones. The brightness of the natural landscape offers much of the color. Within either climate, there will be a period of longer daylight hours and a period of shorter daylight hours as the seasons change.

An additional consideration is whether your living space is in a secluded suburban area or in one with a lot of urban light. In terms of color, an urban environment will be lacking in natural or organic materials and likely have more bright colors with strong chroma. The lighting used for urban applications can also be very bright, with a lot of saturation.

If the space is somewhat contemporary, the stronger colors reflective of the urban environment will play very nicely, and the lighting can be displayed in a more dramatic fashion. A good way to do this is with a combination of direct and indirect light and with a few well-placed bold accents in the artwork or on a wall surface finished with strong color. If you want to balance the brightness of the urban color and light, select color palettes that contain more natural, organic colors and adjust the interior light sources to create more shade and shadow. This is one design area where personal preference prevails.

If you live in a northern climate, you may have fewer windows and shorter days to contend with, which will affect the amount of artificial light you'll need. If this is the case, lighting will be of utmost importance. It may be worth your while to engage the services of a good lighting designer or technician.

A good starting point for lighting design is to determine where your southern exposure is in rela-tion to your living spaces. This is where the direct light will be entering your space, and so it's an important factor if you're interested in creating the look of natural light.

> The most natural way to light a space is to light the walls and objects within a space—not the space itself. The space will seem visually larger, and the shade, shadow, and texture will add visual interest.

Timers are another way to combat the effects of seasonal light. By having a relatively inexpensive timer system installed, different lights can automat-ically come on throughout the day, thus lessening the impact of suddenly walking into a darkened space at 4 o'clock in the afternoon. During times of the year when the days are longer, it is beneficial to have a few areas that are more softly lit, which cre-ates a calmer feeling that sends the psychological signal to wind down from the day. When daylight lasts until 9:00 P.M., the mind oftentimes has diffi-culty relaxing. (See Figure 2.13.)

Figure 2.13 *Whether or not your climate has ice and snow during the winter months, the lower position of the sun in the sky will indicate that it's winter. (Russ Dillingham.)*

Figure 2.14 *This dining and living space is cozy and intimate, but also efficient. The high ceilings add volume, but are not overwhelming because the size of this room is visually altered and balanced by the bookshelves, fireplace mantle, built-in seating, and the suspended light fixtures, which add a human scale to the environment. (Gauthier-Stacy, Inc. Photographer: Greg Premru.)*

Whether you're working toward counterbalancing or enhancing the effects of climate with your design choices, color plays a significant role in the success of the look you're trying to achieve. Either way, seasonal changes for color palettes are easy to affect with the intensity (lightness and darkness), texture, and tone of accessories. For example, if you have floors with area rugs, you can choose simple woven ones or oilcloths for the warmer months and heavier Oriental and wool rugs for the cooler months. You can also choose layered window treatments so you can add or remove pieces as the season dictates.

Color and Dimension

You can visually alter the shape and proportion of a room with color and texture by painting or finishing the walls in different colors with contrasting values. A color scheme using neutral monotone or monochromatic colors creates an open and airy feeling in a small room. In a long and narrow room, painting the shorter walls a dark or darker color than the longer walls can make the room seem wider. A warm color will make objects in a room appear closer, whereas a cool color will make them appear farther away. Contrasting hues, when used together, can create a sense of vibration between the colors. A ceiling can appear to be lower when painted a darker color than the walls. Furniture in the same color as a wall will seem to blend into the wall; however, furniture that contrasts with the wall color will become an accent within the space. The same principles apply to the treatment of architectural elements throughout an interior. (See Figures 2.14 to 2.17.)

Figure 2.15 The contrast of the light furnishings against the dark wall impact the proportion of this reading corner by visually separating it from the outside space. While this is not generally the intent, in a seasonal climate it may be desirable. *(Gauthier-Stacy, Inc. Photographer: Sam Gray.)*

Figure 2.16 The general living area of this space is intended for socializing and circulating, but the dining area has been made more intimate by raising the floor and creating low partitions. *(Andrew Liberty Interiors, IIDA.)*

Figure 2.17 The use of tromp l'oeil on this knee wall adds dimension and depth to this room by visually expanding the view. *(Jane Considine Decorative Painting.)*

Zoning with Color

Using different colors, textures, intensities, and tones can differentiate and demarcate areas within a space. Figures 2.18 through 2.23 demonstrate effective methods for defining living spaces through the use of color, texture, and tone.

Figure 2.18 This colorful storage unit serves a dual purpose, as both a multimedia storage facility and a room divider. *(Braun Design, Ltd., Maura Braun, IIDA. Photo © George Lambrose, Lambrose Photography, Inc.)*

Figure 2.19 This dining space has been made to feel more cozy and intimate by painting the walls a dark color that contrasts with the light hues used in the living room beyond. *(Gill Smith, Interior and Landscape Designer, Aukland, New Zealand.)*

Figure 2.20 The intense tropical tones are confined to the interior spaces, while the patio areas that are open to the exterior have a light and airy quality. This is a very effective transition to the lush greenery of the exterior environment. *(Arq. Diego Matthai, IIDA, Matthai Arquitectos. Photo by Sebastian Saldivar.)*

Figure 2.21 As this photo demonstrates, color and texture work well with neutral palettes. This rock formation was carved by nature and transitions gently to the shoreline as it meets with softly textured grasses. *(Russ Dillingham.)*

Figure 2.22 If you have an open-plan design and find it difficult to define separate areas, the use of an area rug with strong contrast in color and/or texture will define a clear boundary for seating or dining. *(Douglas Kahn/Gould Evans.)*

Figure 2.23 *The use of paint can help to differentiate between spaces and the functions within them. The dining room is a dark green while the hallway finishes are warm rust tones, offsetting the neutral color of the living room. The upholstery colors used on the furnishings and the coordinating wood finishes tie the three spaces together. (Photo by Peter Paige.)*

Creating Depth Illusion with Mirrors

Ever wonder how you can make a small space seem larger or wider? One of the easiest ways to create depth illusion in a room is with mirrors. Mirrors can be used to make a room seem wider or longer, or they can be used to visually double an interesting detail or object. For instance, if you place a mirror on an end wall within a room that seems small or narrow, the room will appear larger.

While windows can bring the outside in and make a room seem wider and more open, creating more windows may not be a viable option. In a room lacking windows, a similar effect can be created with mirrors, glass doors on cabinetry, and accent lighting, as shown in Figures 2.24 through 2.27.

Altering Scale with Accessories and Plants

The size of a room can be enhanced or altered by properly coordinating accessories and plants. If a room has high ceilings, for example, the use of artwork on the walls and tall potted plants can bring a more human scale to the space. Both accessories

Figure 2.24 The triangular-shaped mirror enhances this living room and subtly adds volume to the room. *(Photo by Peter Paige.)*

Figure 2.25 This accent shelf becomes an optical illusion by having the mirror installed floor to ceiling. The shelf and floor finish appear to be doubled, which greatly adds to the perceived volume of this space. *(Tom Gass, IIDA, Gass Design. Photo by Peter Paige.)*

Figure 2.26 Mirrors and light have been well used in this bathroom to create visual interest and volume. A row of mirrors runs continuously along the wall, some intending to reflect the display and toiletry items, others for general use, and the ones at the sink basins angled for more personal viewing. The lighting also is focused on highlighting specific functions and features. Note the cove lighting used in the toe space of the vanity cabinet. *(Lori W. Carroll, ASID, IIDA. William Lesch Photography.)*

Figure 2.27 This room divider has been adorned with art to create a sculptural effect. *(Arq. Diego Matthai, Matthai Arquitectos. Photo by Sebastian Saldivar.)*

and plants can bring color into a space and can be used as the primary focal point of a room. Using an accessory as a primary focal point can be particularly interesting if you have a favorite piece or collector's item. Figures 2.28 through 2.33 exemplify the importance of accessories and plants in altering and enhancing a space.

Figure 2.28 As a room is enhanced with accent colors, these yellow flowers are enhanced by this colorful butterfly. *(Russ Dillingham.)*

Figure 2.29 A monotone color palette is enhanced in this living space with the addition of exciting accessories, textures, and antique furnishings. *(Photo by Peter Paige.)*

Figure 2.30   The artwork in this room not only serves as a backdrop to the office space, it also creates a strong focal point and personalizes the room. The scale of the room is further altered by varying the proportions of the artwork, which balances well with the lightness of the table-style desk. If the designer had used only the smaller prints on the wall, the desk might feel out of proportion with the rest of the room. *(Gauthier-Stacy, Inc. Photographer: Sam Gray.)*

Figure 2.31 This eclectic blend of accessories will allow you to personalize any area of a room. Fresh-cut flowers can help the look to evolve throughout the seasons of the year. *(Tom Gass, IIDA, Gass Design. Photo by Peter Paige.)*

Figure 2.32 This is a very dramatic example of zoning—not only with color, but also with texture, light, and artwork. As you can see, the carpet on the floor has been cut into a pattern that flows from one space to the next, while the lighting has been designed to reflect off of the wall surfaces, to accent the wall mural, and to highlight sculpture. The wall mural adds an exciting visual image of an imaginary skyline, giving the room the feel of being a metropolitan penthouse. This is effective in spaces where there are no appreciable views. *(Tom Gass, IIDA, Gass Design. Photo by Peter Paige.)*

Figure 2.33 This oversized mirror brings much-needed excitement to an otherwise transitional space. It is also a great way to provide a "window" to other views, where no window or view may exist. *(Lori W. Carroll, ASID, IIDA. William Lesch Photography.)*

Summary

With the understanding that the less defined parameters of color selection play a significant role in the creation of our color palettes, we can begin to layer accordingly. We begin with the basics, create our color palettes, add texture, contrast, and light, and really look at the space. Just as we need to fully listen when we work with our clients, we also need to listen to the space, look at the light, ponder what it is we are hoping to achieve, and then do it. Armed with the insight of this chapter, we can move on to some practical considerations for selecting the right finishes and materials for the job.

CHAPTER 3

Practical Considerations: Selecting Materials and Lighting

Once you have a basic understanding of color, color palettes, and the psychological implications of their use, you can begin the process of selecting and using some of the many different materials available. Looking toward specific materials, we start considering the three-dimensional aspects of design more fully. This chapter introduces many of the basics of materials:

- Selecting the right material for the job

- Paint versus wallpaper

- Color and textural variety

- Flooring options

- Lighting options

While the options are almost unlimited, we'll outline an appropriate starting point by presenting the criteria for selecting the right material, and we'll look at a variety of paint, wall coverings, hard finishes (e.g., stone and tile), floor materials, and lighting options. Ultimately, selections will be based on personal preference, but we'll describe the practicality of each material for different applications so that you can make informed decisions.

Selecting the Right Material for the Job

When selecting the right material for the job, it's critical to understand how the space will be used so that the performance of the materials selected and installed will be appropriate for the functions of the space. Consider the following factors:

- How much am I able or willing to spend?

- What is the typical life span of this material?

- What kind of maintenance will be required (if any)?

- Do I prefer hard or soft finishes on my floor?

- Do I want to combine wall or floor materials to visually divide the spaces or create contrast and interest?

In a smaller space with an open floor plan—like a studio space—you may want to define different areas through the use of finish materials. For example, use tile flooring in the kitchen/food-preparation area and hardwood or carpet in the living area. An area rug can be layered over the hardwood to further define a sitting area or dining area. On wall surfaces, paint colors, wall coverings, glass block, wood veneers, or tile can be used to add further definition to the different areas, and, of course, artwork and plants can also be added for this purpose.

- If using wallpaper or vinyl, what widths of rolls are available? If the space has many large areas to be covered, it may be more cost-effective to use wider rolls so there will be fewer seams. If the space is broken up with several doors, windows, openings, and so on, narrower rolls will be easier to install.

- If the wallpaper or vinyl has a pattern or repeat, the size and scale of the space will become a consideration. Larger-scale patterns tend to minimize a space, and you'll need to purchase more rolls of product to match up the pattern with its adjacent strip on the wall.

All finish materials have ratings that reflect their durability. Table 3.1 is a brief guide to material selection based on use.

Of course, there are areas that will fall in between the categories described in Table 3.1, but this is a good general guide for material use.

If you're not installing the product yourself, the installer will want to calculate the amount of paint, vinyl, or wallpaper to be ordered, and it is not uncommon to allow 10 to 15 percent extra for waste. Having leftover paint or wall covering is preferable to having to reorder, since each batch of paint, wall covering, or fabric can vary slightly from other batches, even if the color and pattern are the same.

Material may be selected based on its application alone. For example, when selecting a wall material for the kitchen or bathroom it may not be necessary to have a finish material as durable as tile, stone, or stainless steel on the walls or backsplash, but the practicality of a water-resistant, low-maintenance finish material that can easily be wiped clean makes these materials ideal for kitchens and bathrooms. Remember, a durable and long-lasting finish material that costs more initially may wind up having a lower *life-cycle cost* (what a material costs over a given period of time). The following are some examples of life-cycle costs:

- Paint costs approximately $.50 to $.65 per square foot and lasts 5 years before needing to be touched up. The color options are limited only by your imagination, and it is relatively easy to change colors and to do it yourself.

- A paint-coating system may cost (depending on the pattern selected) approximately $1.00 to $1.50 per square foot and last 8 to 10 years. A paint-coating system is a high-quality, durable paint that is applied with a compressor and sprayer fitted with size-specific nozzles. Several

Table 3.1 *Material Durability Rating*

DENSITY OF MATERIAL:	20 LB OR LESS	20–30 LB	30–40 LB OR GREATER
Light use (usually limited to residential applications)	Paint Grass cloth Wallpaper		
Moderate use (residential and light commercial use)		Paint Medium-weight vinyl Paint-coating systems Sealed woods and veneers	
Heavy use (commercial, industrial, high-traffic spaces)			Paint-coating systems Heavy-weight vinyl Glass blocks Hardwood Tile Stone or masonry Sealed metals

colors of paint with varying densities are sprayed on in one motion, creating multicolored, multi-textured finishes. It's a very versatile option, once reserved only for commercial application, but perfectly appropriate for residential use. It is less expensive than most vinyl, has no seams, and offers unlimited color options. The installation time is similar to that of paint, but must be done by a trained paint contractor licensed to use the product.

- Vinyl or wallpaper may cost approximately (depending on the pattern and weight selected) $1 to $2 per square foot and last 10 to 12 years. Unless you're skilled in hanging wallpaper or vinyl, you'll want to consult with a trained professional for guidance. Vinyl is generally considered to be more durable than paint and offers many different textures and effects. Wallpaper is less durable than vinyl, but offers much greater versatility in style and appearance.

- Tile or stone can cost approximately $2 to $10 per square foot and up and will generally last 20 years or more. Because it holds up so well, you'll want to consider factors beyond life-cycle cost. Depending on your personal preferences, tile work that's very stylized or trendy can look out of date or out of fashion long before it wears out. If you're renovating a large space and plan to sell, select tile that is a neutral or classic color such as black, white, ivory, terra-cotta, beige, or grey. If the tiled area is small, you have more latitude with color and pattern because it won't be too expensive to change it when styles change. Using a neutral or classic color on the floor and adding accent tiles on the wall places the visual interest closer to eye level, where it can be better appreciated.

Again, this is only a general guide, and we cannot emphasize enough that the cost will vary greatly according to quality and style selected and the region in which you live. Another variable cost is labor, which differs from one installer to another and from one geographic region to another. Some installers are highly skilled artisans, specializing in one type of installation, and will likely be more expensive to hire. If the finish materials being installed are very distinctive and/or the space is difficult (uneven surfaces, irregular shapes or angles), it may be well worth spending more on the installation. If, however, the installation of materials is very simple and straightforward, select an installer with more versatility. Of course, if you choose to do your own painting, tile work, and so on, the cost will be less. In some instances, you'll be able to afford a more expensive product by installing it yourself, and many building material suppliers may be willing to assist you in determining quantities, providing many of the tools needed for the project, and/or providing detailed installation instructions to get the job done.

Materials for Small Spaces

When a space has limited square footage, selecting materials becomes a little more complicated. Here are a few tips to keep in mind:

- Patterns matter. It's best to use small-scale patterns. That doesn't mean you can't use large-scale patterns at all, however. Try to keep the majority of patterns smaller in scale, then use larger patterns in accent pieces such as an area rug, a piece of artwork, or decorative pillows.

- Limit the use of darker values and hues. While darker colors are not taboo, their use should be limited. Too many dark colors can make a small space feel very cavelike. Unless this is your objective, try to balance darker colors with lighter trim and accessories. Also, remember to provide plenty of additional lighting if there is little natural light available.

- Balance floor, wall, and ceiling colors. Concentrating dark colors at the end of a long room will make it appear shorter; a dark ceiling will look lower; a dark floor will seem heavier. If the room or space is small, keep the ceiling color light (light fixtures directed at the ceiling will also enhance ceiling height), and steer toward lighter tones on the walls and floor. Bring darker colors into the palette with area rugs, art, accessories, and window treatments.

- If the ceiling is relatively low, or you simply want it to appear higher, try installing your drapery hardware as close to the ceiling as possible, creating a longer vertical line down the wall in the drapery fabric. If you do this, make sure your drapery valance or swag covers to the top of the window opening. Another advantage of this trick is that, because the drapery starts higher, it doesn't need to cover as much of the window opening, so more natural light can be made available.

- Lighting, lighting, lighting. As mentioned, directing as much light as possible onto the ceiling will make it seem higher. Also, try flooding, or directing more light, into corners and onto walls. The technique of locating light fixtures close to walls or objects so that they light the surface horizontally or vertically is called *grazing*.

- Mirrors can greatly enhance the scale of a space, but don't overdo it. By positioning a framed mirror over a storage cabinet, above fireplace mantle, or in a corridor, you can visually double the space. If you are considering a mirror, pay attention to the area of the room that will be reflected, and whether that area itself needs special attention to color or detail. If there's a great architectural detail opposite the mirror, its reflection can be a very striking addition to the room, whereas if the area reflected in the mirror is cluttered, the opposite will be true. Again, don't overuse mirrors, because the result can be very disorienting to the occupants.

As these tips illustrate, balance and moderation are the keys to using materials successfully in a small space. There are no absolute dos or don'ts; as you select materials, stay focused on your objective for the finished product.

Using Paint and Wallpaper

Both paint and wallpaper can give a room textural interest. Using them together—for example, divided by a chair rail on a wall—can bring a traditional, a contemporary, or an eclectic flair to a space, de-pending on the colors, patterns of wallpaper, or textures used. Paint is the least-expensive way to bring color to a space, while wall coverings can vary greatly in price. Using a combination of paint and wall covering is an excellent way to add character and distinction to your space as economically as possible. Figure 3.1 illustrates the use of several subtle colors, large-scaled artwork, and mirrors to give visual interest to the space. Note that most of the light fixtures direct brightness at the ceiling, corners, and walls. This very effective use of light makes the space seem larger than it actually is. (See Figures 3.2 to 3.4.)

Figure 3.1   Diversity with the use of paint selections can give a room character without the use of wallpaper. *(Photo by Peter Paige.)*

Figure 3.2 This bathroom illustrates how integrating paint and wallpaper can add richness, color, and textural qualities to a room. At the sink vanity, tile is a practical embellishment. *(Photo by Peter Paige.)*

Figure 3.3 The wall finish used in this space integrates the artwork successfully while enhancing the monotone color palette. *(Gayle Reynolds, ASID, IIDA. Steve Vierra Photography.)*

Figure 3.4 *The toile design of this wall mural is a great option for wallpaper when you want to adjust the scale of the pattern or can't find the exact color match you need for your palette. (Jane Considine Decorative Painting.)*

Using Color and Textural Variety

By using color and texture together, you can add shadow, dimension, contrast, and balance to a space. Figures 3.5 through 3.15 demonstrate the use of one or all of these principles. In some cases, the simplicity of the space is enhanced, while in others, the period or style is further defined.

Flooring Options

When planning a color palette, we often recommend starting with the floor finishes since fewer color options will be available for flooring, and depending on the space, it can have the most impact. If the space is somewhat open, as in a loft or studio, it will be one of the largest surfaces to cover. If the space is more compartmentalized, with sev-

eral small areas, you may have the option to change finishes from area to area. Either way, it makes sense to start from the ground up.

Hardwood

One of the most versatile flooring options is hardwood. In many older buildings and dwellings, wood is often the original flooring substrate and can be suitable for refinishing or painting, depending on its condition.

Of the hardwoods available, some of the most common are ash, maple, oak, cherry, mahogany, and black walnut. Within these species of wood, each has many varieties with distinct characteristics, depending on the geographical origins. Cherry, for example, has two primary varieties—American

Figure 3.5 The branches in a simple vase give the wall covering in this room a three-dimensional quality. This visual play of depth will make a small space seem larger. *(Gauthier-Stacy, Inc. Photographer: Sam Gray.)*

Figure 3.6 The textural variety of the upholstery fabrics and area rug used in this living/dining space contribute beautifully to this neutral color palette. *(Gauthier-Stacy, Inc. Photographer: Sam Gray.)*

Figure 3.7 This entry space owes its success to the combination of texture on the walls, lush greenery, and the bouquet of flowers, all of which contribute to the variety and balance of the space. *(Lori W. Carroll, ASID, IIDA. William Lesch Photography.)*

Figure 3.8 This bedroom shows a great example of the use of neutral palettes, which offer wonderful versatility and help the space seem larger. The walls, floor covering, artwork, mirror, and accessories are all of a coordinating palette, while the visual interest has been created by the bedding, which can be easily redone anytime the occupant wants to refresh the look. *(Lori W. Carroll, ASID, IIDA. William Lesch Photography.)*

Figures 3.9 and 3.10 The simplicity of these spaces is enhanced with the multiuse of texture, as shown in the seating, carpeting, accessories, and geometric shapes of the occasional tables. When trying to make the most of a space, this is a very effective approach. *(Lori W. Carroll, ASID, IIDA. William Lesch Photography.)*

Figure 3.11 This wall detail displays art and is also artwork in itself. The designer has cleverly carved niches that provide visual interest, then finished the wall with a rich, natural, textured tone resembling cork. The flow that results can be very effective in achieving a greater sense of space, in contrast to a more rectilinear layout. *(Michael Spillers/Gould Evans.)*

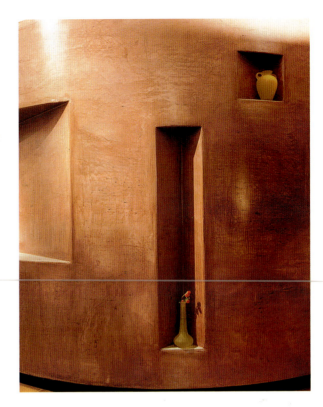

Figure 3.12 A blend of color and textural variety through the use of subdued tones can provide a very classic flair. *(Photo by Peter Paige.)*

Figure 3.13 *The intense reds and blues balance this living room. The use of textures, as in the upholstery, the window treatments, and the Oriental rug, give dimension to this living room. (Photo by Peter Paige.)*

cherry and Brazilian cherry. American cherry wood, grown primarily in North America, is less dense, or hard, than Brazilian cherry (from Brazil). Of the two varieties, the Brazilian cherry is about twice as dense as the American cherry and is likely to hold up to heavier abuse than the American variety. American cherry is also lighter in color and has greater variation in character. Typically, the darker the color of the wood, as it pertains to a particular species, the harder the wood. Hardness, or density, is important for several reasons:

- Harder wood is more durable.

- Harder wood is more stable dimensionally, which means it will be less prone to warping, shrinking, or cupping after it's installed.

- Harder wood gives a more uniform appearance.

Another important characteristic you'll want to be aware of is how the wood is cut from the log into the floor material. Most woods are cut with *plain-* or *flat-sawn* methods, which results in the grain of the wood running across the width of the board. For more stable wood materials, look for wood materials that are *quartersawn,* or *quartered,* which results in a board whose grain runs perpendicular to the face, or thickness, of the board. Because wood expands and contracts as its moisture content changes from season to season, if the grain or rings are running perpendicular, only the thickness is affected. If the grain or rings are running across the width of the board, then the material will change in length and width.

Figure 3.14 *Color repetition and textural variety can balance a space, as shown in this dining room. Painted textures, such as the walls resembling stone in this dining space, give the occupant a greater sense of mass than a flat-textured wall would. (Photo by Peter Paige.)*

One of the greatest aspects of wood floorings' versatility is the ability to mix different woods to create unique and unusual patterns. Patterns can be created by combining contrasting colors of wood such as ash or maple with mahogany or walnut. If you want to do an intricate pattern, there are many exotic woods to select from, such as wenge, purpleheart, and bird's-eye maple. In a smaller space, the lighter wood tones, such as ash, American cherry, maple, and white oak, can help to enhance the spaciousness of your rooms. Also, if the room sizes are irregular, it can be difficult to find proportional area rugs. If that's the case, a wood floor with a contrasting border and another pattern in the center of the room can create the look and interest of a patterned carpet.

When considering wood as a flooring option, you will need to contact a local supplier or installer, because availability and cost will depend on where you live and which species and varieties are most readily available in that region. You'll also want to discuss finish options based on your own lifestyle. If wood is your choice, anticipate spending anywhere from $10 to $20 per square foot with installation—and more if the installation is complex or includes intricate patterns or borders.

Ceramic, Porcelain, Quarry, and Stone Materials

For floors that demand the highest level of durability, you may want to consider tile or stone products.

Figure 3.15 *Visual diversity is demonstrated in this contemporary, chic living space. The designer has skillfully combined warm and cool palettes, achieving balance by using texture and splashes of bold primaries on the warm scale. (Photo by Peter Paige.)*

They're durable, come in a multitude of sizes and thicknesses for varying applications, have great color palette options, and allow the greatest flexibility for creating patterns and designs on walls and floors. If the room you're finishing is small, try using smaller-size tile to make the space look larger in contrast. As with wood floor materials, many patterns, borders, and accent tiles are available in a variety of sizes to create visual interest in areas where an area rug may not be practical. Remember, with all tile and stone products, you must have a structurally solid floor or wall substrate prior to any installation. If you're uncertain about the substrate, check with a licensed professional before proceeding. Following is an overview of the different tile and stone products:

- *Ceramic tile.* This type of tile consists of a baked ceramic or porcelain material that is then glazed on its finish side (the side that will be visible after installation) to provide a waterproof surface. Though not as durable as quarry tile, ceramic tile comes in various thicknesses for different applications. The thinnest, approximately $\frac{1}{8}$ inch, is suitable only for wall surfaces.

- *Porcelain tile.* Similar to ceramic and quarry tile but harder and, unlike glazed tile, the color and/or pattern that you see on the surface goes all the way through the tile. It's a very durable surface, suitable for the same applications as marble and granite. Finishes generally include split stone, smooth with slip resistance, smooth, and polished. If safety and slip resistance are a concern, avoid the smooth and polished surfaces.

- *Quarry tile.* These are tiles of baked clay that can be left in their natural finish to be sealed after installation or glazed for various aesthetic looks. Glazed quarry tile often has texture that adds to both visual interest and slip resistance. It's one of the most durable tiles, but must have a solid substrate for installation. As with stone, it is not suitable for applications where the subfloor is not structurally strong and level.

- *Stone.* This category includes brick, slate, marble, and travertine. Dimensional thickness and density make these heavy materials to install, so they aren't appropriate for every project. Additional structure may be needed for the subfloor prior to installation, which is not always possible. It's best to install this type of material when you have slab-on-grade construction, concrete, or some other structural subfloor. Always consult a licensed professional skilled in structural evaluations.

As with most specialty or hard goods, prices range widely and will depend greatly on where you live. Anticipate $10 to $30 per square foot.

Carpet

Carpet is the quintessential soft flooring option. It provides comfort underfoot, and if the flooring substrate is irregular, it will hide a multitude of sins. Most residential carpeting is installed over a foam or dense mineral-fiber pad to add softness and to prolong the wear of the carpet. Carpet consists of a synthetic nylon or polyurethane fiber, a synthetic blend of fibers, or natural wool fiber that is then either tufted or woven onto a polypropylene or jute surface that becomes its backing. Additional backings, dyes, cutting, and so forth are then added to produce different styles and quality levels of carpet. Carpet is generally manufactured in 12-foot-wide rolls in 60-foot lengths and either tacked or glued down directly on the floor surface. A *rug* refers to a piece of carpet that is not attached directly to the floor, so it can be moved. An *area rug* generally refers to the function of creating a specific space such as a sitting area or a dining area, but is essentially the same as any rug. A small rug used throughout a space would be called a *scatter rug.* The types of carpeting available are too numerous to detail here; however, the following is a general guide:

- Wall-to-wall carpet is the staple of the rug industry and consists of any one or combination of materials such as nylon, polyurethane, or wool. It is tufted on a large factory loom for the purpose of providing a large quantity of carpet in a multitude of styles and colors in a fairly consistent and inexpensive fashion. Some common styles are shag, cut pile, level and multiloops, and Berbers. They're installed over the entire floor area (from wall to wall) and can be installed directly on the floor or over a foam or dense mineral-fiber pad. If the floor is uneven or imperfect, wall-to-wall carpet is a great solution. It's relatively inexpensive and provides the greatest amount of softness, slip resistance, and reduction of foot noise and furniture movement. The biggest disadvantage is that, because carpeting is absorbent, it can hold soiling and stains, which can become unsanitary over time. The other disadvantage is the carpet fiber itself, which can wear and flatten down in the course of a few years, causing the carpet to look old and visually unappealing. Even though some newer fibers have reduced these problems, wall-to-wall carpet is less permanent than a solid finish.

- Typical rugs and area rugs include Orientals, Persians, dhurries, and sisals. They come in various sizes and have finished edges, sometimes fringed, so that they may lie on top of a finished floor. The various names refer to the point of origin and pattern of the rug. Most are made in the Far East and are produced by knotting or tying the yarn onto a backing material. High-quality rugs have as many as 800 knots per square inch. The ends of the knots are then cut to provide a softer pile surface or left as knots for a more durable surface. High-quality cut pile Oriental rugs have a velvety appearance, whereas those with fewer knots per square inch will have more surface texture. Some Oriental rugs that are woven without knotting are called *kilims, soumaks,* and *cashmeres.* They're thinner and lighter than the knotted Orientals, but very durable. Most Oriental rugs are made of natural fibers and materials such as wool, jute, hemp, silk, and cotton, but some machine-made rugs use synthetic materials to produce less-expensive varieties. All of these types of rugs can be either hand- or machine-made, but the hand-knotted or woven varieties are much more distinctive and expensive.

- Carpet tile is a newer form of carpeting in which the carpet material is attached to a heavier backing and cut into smaller units such as 6-foot rolls, 12×12 inch squares, or 18×18 inch squares. The purpose is to provide easier installation with less waste and to allow the customer to replace worn, stained, or damaged areas individually, as needed. Carpet tiles come with several backing options for different levels of durability, softness, static control, and ease of removal. The biggest disadvantages are that they tend to be expensive and they show seams (undesirable if you want a uniform surface).

When considering the purchase of any carpet or rug, you need to ask yourself the following questions:

- Am I going to build the color palette from colors in the carpet, or is the carpet going to be a neutral base that will allow me to add color in other areas of the room?

- Is the rug going to accent my color scheme?

- Will this rug likely be replaced every 5 or 10 years?

- What's my budget?

- How much foot traffic will the rug need to withstand?

Area rugs can be treated as a seasonal accessory or used to add texture and/or color to a space. Persian and Oriental rugs usually work well in spaces located in cooler climates, since they tend to give a sense of warmth and heaviness, whereas sisal, jute, or more brightly colored patterns generally work well in warmer climates, where we think of the cool surface and lightness inherent in their material.

The answers to these questions should dictate both the color and quality of the area rug you're considering for purchase. If the rug will be a serious investment, the quality should be higher, and the construction and yarn dye methods should be of a high caliber. In a smaller space, a smaller-scale area rug will have a greater opportunity to stand out as a feature of your color palette. We recommend selecting classic color palettes that are not likely to become dated or fall out of fashion. A few color palettes are considered to be classic in the rug industry, such as Oriental reds, navy blues, tea-stained ivory and gold tones, and emerald and sage greens. These classic colors have been the standard palettes in Oriental rugs because of the dyes originally available. Although the color options are much wider now, most rooms will easily accommodate one of these classic colors when woven into the right style of rug. If the carpet will be replaced more frequently, you have much greater flexibility with color and style choices.

If carpet is your surface of choice, plan to spend $15 to $60 per square yard depending on thickness, style, and material. For Orientals and other distinctive area rugs, the price range is too large to list. If an Oriental is out of your price range, consider having a piece of carpet that suits your style cut to the size you want and edged with a carpet-finishing material so that you can use it as an area rug. This is a good option in a smaller space where the size you need isn't readily available. It's also a good solution if you have a hard-surface floor in a room such as a bedroom and you want to add warmth and softness underfoot without carpeting the entire room. Whether your space is large or small, carpet and area rugs can add softness, definition, texture, and visual interest to your floor, regardless of your budget.

Resilient Flooring

Resilient flooring materials include vinyl (PVC) or rubber sheet flooring and tiles, vinyl composition tiles (VCT), linoleum, and cork. One of the most useful properties of resilient floor products is that they're easy to work into a small space. In tile form, they can be easily fitted into tight spaces, and with all of the color and pattern options, you can create virtually any look you want on the floor without spending a lot of money.

- Of the vinyl and rubber varieties, rubber is more expensive, but it is also much more durable and resilient, which is also why it's often added to vinyl products to enhance their overall performance. The higher the rubber content, the higher the cost and the greater the durability.

- Linoleum is a sheet vinyl that's become popular again due to its high durability and its greatly improved color selection.

- Most of these products have a homogeneous property, meaning that the color and/or pattern are continuous through its thickness. If the floor is scratched or chipped, the color will remain the same. There are lesser-quality sheet vinyl products on the market that have the color and pattern only on the surface, which are suitable only for areas with very little traffic, such as a residential lavatory. If the area to be surfaced demands a highly durable covering, you should use only those with the homogeneous property.

- Homogeneous sheet vinyl, rubber, and linoleum can be installed with all seams heat-welded so that the surface of the floor is monolithic and watertight.

- Cork is a renewable natural material that offers many of the aesthetic qualities of a wood floor, but is more resilient underfoot. A large part of the world's supply of cork comes from Portugal, where it's harvested from the bark of the cork oak tree during the summer months when the tree dehydrates and its outer bark becomes loose. The bark of the cork oak replenishes itself every 9 years, and no harm comes to the tree as a result of the harvesting. After harvest, it's manufactured into many styles, colors, patterns, and thicknesses, and it comes in a variety of finishes such as sanded, waxed, polyurethaned, and vinyl coated. It installs more easily than wood, because it installs with glue instead of nails and the material is easier to cut and scribe around tight spaces. It's also significantly lighter in weight, so it doesn't need the structural subfloor required of tile and stone floors.

As with most floor materials, cost will vary widely depending on material, pattern, quantity, and local labor installation costs. Anticipate $3 to $7 per square foot for vinyl and rubber and $10 to $15 for cork. (See Figure 3.16.)

Figure 3.16 *This whimsical tile design forces the eye to explore. The designer has found a way to have fun with asymmetry. By placing randomly patterned tile within a field of solid-colored tile, a greater sense of space is achieved. (Diana Bennett Wirtz, ASID, Amethyst Design.)*

Faux Finishes

Another option for flooring is the use of faux finishes. Reasons to opt for faux finishing vary greatly and include the following:

- There may be a lack of desirable floor material. Often, in smaller spaces, every inch counts, so when a floor material is relatively smooth but not aesthetically appealing, painting it is a good solution. Painting has the added benefit of eliminating the need to layer additional material on top of the existing floor. A *faux finish* is a fake finish that resembles another material—usually a more expensive material like marble or stone—which allows you to affordably achieve almost any look you want. It could be an intricate mosaic or, as shown in Figures 3.17 and 3.18, a 12-inch-square black-and-white marble tile floor. The scale of the tile you choose should be proportionate to the size of the room. If the

room is large, a pattern that uses larger blocks of the same-color tile alternating with patterned or accenting tiles will help to balance the volume of space. A smaller room will feel more in proportion with tiles that are 12 inches square or less.

- The area may be inappropriate for real marble. Highly polished marble is beautiful, but it's very slippery, requires ongoing maintenance (marble can often become stained, even when sealed), and is very expensive. A faux finish has the look of marble but retains the texture of the underlying floor material, which is likely to be less slippery. In addition, the faux-finished floor will be more resistant to staining than marble and won't need to be polished and buffed on a regular basis. It is, however, less durable than natural stone.

- In some situations, natural materials such as marble or granite are too heavy. If there's any question regarding the stability of the structure, you need to consult a licensed professional skilled in evaluating structure before installing a heavy flooring.

- You may want to achieve a whimsical feel for the space.

- A faux area rug or oilcloth is a very practical solution for a dining area because it eliminates the worry of soiling or staining a beautiful, expensive area rug.

- Unlike an area rug, you cannot trip on a faux rug.

- It may be less expensive than the material it represents. Even though faux finishing is not always less expensive, it may be more practical in some situations.

Figures 3.17 and 3.18 The use of color blocking (a pattern of contrasting colors) on this classic black-and-white floor design creates an excellent pathway in this entrance area. *(Jane Considine Decorative Painting.)*

Lighting Options

Lighting can be one of the most creative components of design. Let's say, for example, you have a narrow corridor. The most effective way to light it would be to flood one or both walls with light. The light would then reflect off of the wall, creating very dramatic ambient light and effectively widening the appearance of the corridor. *Ambient light,* also called *indirect light,* is a softer level of light that results when light fixtures are aimed toward a wall, a ceiling, or an object, filling the space with reflected light. It's a very good option for a corridor or for any area that does not require task lighting. The more light you can provide in an indirect manner, the better, because it's easy on the eyes, has no glare, and can offer the added benefit of illuminating artwork or other decorative elements on the wall. Indirect lighting is also an effective way to showcase the color or texture of a wall because, by directing the light up, down, or along a wall, any texture on the wall will be enhanced. Conversely, ambient lighting is not a good option for a wall has a lot of damage, since it will bring more attention to it.

Recessed fixtures (sometimes referred to as *recessed can lights*) are lights that are installed above the ceiling line so that they don't protrude below the surface. They should be positioned 12 to 24 inches from the wall to the center of the fixture and spaced anywhere from 3 to 4 feet apart. They are most widely available with incandescent, fluorescent, and halogen lamping and are used for general overall light, accent light, wall washing, and spotlighting. Recessed lighting is a good option for a small space because it doesn't take up additional room and doesn't detract from more interesting features of your space that you prefer to enhance, such as artwork.

Track lights are fixtures that are installed on the surface of a wall or ceiling, where the wiring for the individual fixture(s) is in the track and the lights are positioned on the track. Track lighting can be mounted directly to the wall or ceiling surface and can also be dropped below the ceiling similar to a pendant fixture. The advantages of track lighting are that it can be installed in an area without access to wiring in the wall or ceiling or in an area without enough depth to install a recessed fixture, and it allows the user to aim the individual track lights wherever lighting is desired. Track lighting comes in a variety of styles and sizes to suit most periods of design. There are many traditional styles of track heads available, and a simple, small-scaled track light with no cover can be appropriate in any style of space. Track lights are often used in more-contemporary spaces, but because of their flexibility, we recommend their use in nearly any style of setting. Track lighting can be used both as direct and indirect light and can be lamped with incandescent and halogen light bulbs.

Pendants are light fixtures that hang down from the ceiling line and can range from large chandelier-type fixtures often seen in foyers or dining spaces to smaller, multiple-lamp fixtures. The type of lamping for residential application can be virtually any type available, such as incandescent, fluorescent, fiber-optic, halogen, or low-voltage halogen. The types of shade or housing can be designed to direct light down only, up only, up and down, or open for all-around light distribution. Pendants are a great way to accent a space and add distinction and opulence, but are less desirable if you do not want to see the fixture in your sight line.

Sconces provide the most decorative touch of all, with a vast variety of styles and lamp options, but may not be suited for very narrow or low-ceiling corridors because of their size. Most sconces protrude too far into the corridor, and they can become a hazard if the corridor is narrow and the sconce is located at a height where people could bump their heads. The Americans with Disabilities Act (ADA) governs the maximum depth and mounting height for wall sconces (or any fixture mounted on the wall) to prevent this from becoming a problem. Check with your local code enforcement officials for up-to-date criteria.

For a warmer, more subdued effect, use incandescent bulbs. For a brighter, clearer white light, halogen is the right choice. Halogen also has more flexibility with the size (width and length) of the light beam that projects from it, and the lamps are available in a wide range of wattages (brightness). This is an important feature if you want to create a sharper, narrower beam of light on the wall to spotlight an object without purchasing a special fixture specifically designed to direct its light toward the wall. The wider the spread of the beam, the more uniform and even the overall light will be. If the space is very small, and all or most of the light comes from recessed light fixtures, it's more visually interesting to use more indirect (ambient) light. If the space will also have other types of light, such as floor or table lamps, sconces, or track, then a light fixture near the centerline of the room with a wider beam may be more suitable. Another advantage of halogen light is its crispness which will visually make any space feel larger. Again, lighting choices are all relative to the size and function of the space—a circulation area such as a corridor or vestibule will need less light than a kitchen or bathroom. If you're uncertain about what type of fixture you need, consult a professional lighting consultant or designer who can help you with fixture types, placement, and quantities.

Using light to play up a focal object (fireplace, artwork, vase, plant, or other accessory) is a good design option to explore. By highlighting a few strategically placed items, you add visual interest and successfully play up a strong color or texture to its greatest advantage.

Fixture options for highlighting include lamps for low-voltage spotlighting, wall washing, indirect lighting, and the use of feature lights. One of the greatest advantages to highlighting is that it allows you to control the shade and shadow effects of lighting in a space. If too much artificial light is from indirect or ambient sources, the space becomes too evenly lit and can be psychologically disorienting to the occupants. The eye needs to perceive depth, and the shadows that highlighting provides do just that. (See Table 3.2.)

Controls and Timers

Final lighting issues to consider are controls and timers. Timers simply are clocks that can be set to turn a light fixture on and off at designated times.

Table 3.2 Light Fixtures

TYPE OF FIXTURE	TYPICAL APPLICATIONS
Recessed can lights	Corridors, hallways, kitchen counters, general overall light (residential)
Track lighting	Accent lighting, artwork, areas without existing wiring in the wall or where wiring is difficult to reach
Wall sconces, surface-mounted fixtures	Corridors, passageways, decorative lighting such as flanking a fireplace, doorway, or object, general overall lighting
Low-voltage lights	Accent light, highlighting an object or small area
Wall washers, spotlights	Lighting artwork, lighting walls or other objects
Pendant lights	Decorative light over a table or counter, general overall lighting

Controls are master-switch systems that allow you to turn one or many lights on and off at different times and to adjust lighting levels throughout a house or apartment with dimmers. These systems are often set up with one or two master-switch locations, such as the entry and the master bedroom, and they are generally designed to work with timers, but have manual override if you want to adjust the lighting at any time. They can even be set up so that various lights are on at the same time for different purposes, such as one setting for entertaining, one for earlier in the day, and another for late at night. Some systems are even equipped with remote controls so that occupants can turn on a series of lights that will light their way into and through the house from a remote location such as the driveway. The options are unlimited, and the cost will be based on the complexity of the individual system. Control systems are generally used in larger settings, but a smaller space can also benefit from the additional security provided by keeping the home or apartment looking more lived in when lights come on and off randomly. (See Figures 3.19 to 3.25.)

Figure 3.19 The designer has achieved a theatrical, techno-look by using additive color to complement this neutral contrasting color scheme. (Doreen LeMay Madden; LUX Lighting Design.)

Figures 3.20 and 3.21 The architect has cleverly created the illusion of added space and natural light sources by using textured glass panels with backlighting. *(Designer: Lance Hosey, AIA. Photography by Robert Kassabian.)*

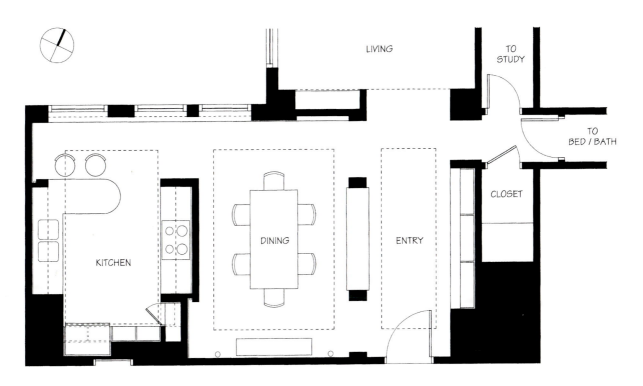

Figure 3.22 The designer has used a backlighting technique on the far wall, which becomes a unique and effective way to highlight this room. *(Lori W. Carroll, ASID, IIDA. William Lesch Photography.)*

Figure 3.23 These whimsical figures are a way to bring light and energy into this space. *(Douglas Kahn/Gould Evans.)*

Figure 3.24 This dining space demonstrates excellent use of low-voltage lighting techniques. Pinhole downlights illuminate the dining table, while suspended track lights accent the artwork. The overall impact is striking and dynamic. *(Arq. Diego Matthai, IIDA, Matthai Arquitectos. Photo by Sebastian Saldivar.)*

Summary

With the myriad of principles and guidelines for selecting materials and lighting, the art of color and design becomes more precise. Successful design doesn't happen by accident. Experience makes the process easier, but even professional designers who continue to explore find that the options are nearly infinite. The following chapters will take you on a tour of some of the work that results when designers and architects reach above and beyond the simple principles of color and design.

Figure 3.25 The suspended low-voltage accent light enhances the abstract quality of the art. The highly reflective surfaces in the room further enhance the overall brightness of the light. *(Arq. Diego Matthai, IIDA, Matthai Arquitectos. Photo by Sebastian Saldivar.)*

PART 2

Multifunction Spaces

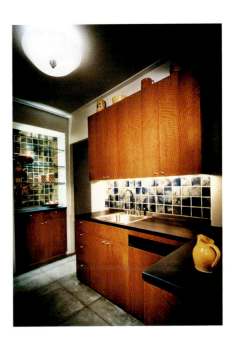

CHAPTER 4
Studio and Loft Spaces

As we begin our foray into specific types of living spaces, we start with the quintessential multiuse spaces known as studios and lofts. We'll explore demarcation of areas, function, and architectural elements.

When we think of living and working within the same space, studio and loft spaces automatically come to mind. The term *studio* generally refers to a small, one-room living space, whereas a *loft* is generally larger, with a higher ceiling where additional floor area can be constructed. Many lofts were the upper level of commercial and industrial buildings considered unsuitable for workspace because of sloping ceiling lines that left some exterior walls less than full height. In both studios and lofts, the living space is quite open, with ancillary spaces such as bathrooms and kitchens being consolidated together, allowing the resident many options for laying out and dividing the space. Historically, studio and loft spaces were large open spaces occupied by artists and dancers who needed large uncluttered space to work. They were often located in industrial areas or in barns and finished in white, off-white, or neutral color palettes so as not to distract artists from their work. The functional part of the living space was simple, basic, and limited to only what was necessary. For the purposes of this chapter, we'll assume the more modern concept of a studio or loft as small, open, utilitarian living space.

Demarcating Areas: Multiuses in a Single Space

In studio and loft spaces, separation of the living, dining, cooking, and sleeping spaces can be accomplished with color, furniture placement, area rugs, changes in light levels, and plants. (See Figures 4.1 and 4.2.)

Try creating cozy niches for quieter functions—such as sleeping or curling up with a good book—by painting these areas warm, deep-hued colors and lighting the spaces softly with indirect and task light for reading. Finish by furnishing with soft materials and pillows for comfort.

Figure 4.1   The built-in bookcases and the area rug are subtle ways to demarcate this open space. The natural light enhances the serene color palette. *(Gayle Reynolds, ASID, IIDA. Photo © Eric Roth.)*

The original intent of studio living was to work and live within the same space. Figure 4.3 and most of the figures throughout this chapter are wonderful examples of creative, open living spaces, demonstrating how a wide variety of themes can be effectively achieved in a studio space.

Figure 4.2 This open area is separated with a glass-topped storage unit that also becomes an architectural element. *(Designer: Lance Hosey, AIA. Photography by Robert Kassabian.)*

Figure 4.3 This is a creative demonstration of how an open space can be arranged for multiuse living. The touches of color on the furnishings, the valance over the door, the pendant lighting, and the flowers are all subtle ways of defining space. The walls and flooring are soft, subtle tones that don't detract from the movable elements of the room and are typical of studio and loft spaces. *(Braun Design, Ltd., Maura Braun, IIDA. Photo © George Lambrose, Lambrose Photography, Inc.)*

Using a Traditional Style in Multiuse Spaces

While many older industrial buildings were devoid of details we consider aesthetically pleasing, there are certainly some beautiful exceptions, especially in historical areas. Some of the most common details are exposed brick and block walls, glass block exterior walls, beautiful brick or stone archways separating open spaces, concrete and wood floors, and sometimes wood or tin ceilings. More intricate features include valances and crown mouldings, curve-topped and transom windows, and occasionally some old plumbing or light fixtures that are still functional. If your intent is to create an authentic traditional design, remember that simply having traditional color palettes and antique fixtures may not be enough. In old, renovated buildings, systems like plumbing and electricity had to be added. They were not neatly tucked into walls, ceilings, and floor plenums. To achieve a traditional design, consider keeping or adding elements such as the following:

- Raised platforms under bathtubs

- Pull-chain lavatory fixtures

- Radiator boxes and window seats to conceal newly installed pipe and ductwork

- Surface-mounted and pendant light fixtures

- Freestanding kitchen cabinetry and cooking areas

You can still have all of the modern conveniences in a traditional space. The features listed here are just some of the details you may want to consider incorporating into your design to create a more authentic feel.

To understand the evolution of color as it applies to our homes, it's helpful to first look at the history of exterior color, because that's where first impressions are established.

In the 1800s, we had neoclassical colors like yellowish white, ivory tones, grey-greens, blue-greys, and tans that were intended to simulate the stone and marble architecture of the ancient Greek and Roman structures. In the early twentieth century, classical gold trimmed with white was very fashionable, and dark muted green became a popular shutter color because it emulated the weathered-bronze shutters of Renaissance buildings. The mid-1800s were about moving from Greek Revival toward Gothic Revival with warmer palettes of earth-toned colors. By the late 1800s, new pigments were becoming available that offered brighter, more colorful palettes, and we began to see the Victorian style emerge (named for Queen Victoria, who was very fond of the new rose and lavender shades). The industrial revolution rejoiced in the bright, slick colors that were newly available. By the 1900s, darker pigments such as browns, olives, reds, and oranges were often used on buildings to give them a greater sense of mass and grandeur. Many older Victorian buildings applied several of these colors to the exterior of a building to accentuate the complexity of its architecture.

The early to mid-1900s brought the Arts and Crafts movement, which sought to bring simplicity and organics back to our structures. These artisans, architects, and furniture designers revived many of the earth-toned colors that had been abandoned during the Victorian era, and their buildings and interior spaces had a quiet, utilitarian efficiency about them. By the mid- to late 1900s, we had access to virtually every color in the rainbow, had weathered many economic ups and downs, and had witnessed several more evolutions of architectural style.

Today, due to rising costs of construction, many of our living spaces are smaller. Many of the lofts and studios of yesterday have been broken down into smaller lofts and studios. For traditional color palettes, we suggest complementary palettes using deep hues with coordinating accents. Trim should be kept to a white or off-white. Wood finishes should be medium to dark tones of mahogany or cherry, but can also include other woods. An example of a traditional color palette might be hunter green and burgundy, with accents of gold and navy blue, and cream-colored trim at the windows and doors. Another example of a traditional palette is sky blue with rich gold hues, accented with sage green and apricot and white trim. The accent colors can be added through floral arrangements, plants, artwork, area rugs, and upholstery. (See Figures 4.4 to 4.6.)

Using a Contemporary Style in Multiuse Spaces

While many studio or loft spaces are located in old buildings, most are devoid of rich architectural embellishments. In their place are exposed pipes and ductwork on the walls and ceilings, exposed brick or block walls, and floors of concrete or wood. These spaces also often have support columns of steel encased in concrete, with no aesthetic detail, which may be awkwardly positioned in the center of the space or between window openings. When this is the case, a contemporary style works very well. These unembellished elements can be painted the same color as nearby walls so that they're less noticeable. If you're trying

Figure 4.4 A street view of this renovated apartment hints at the palette of colors to be revealed inside. (Arq. Diego Matthai, IIDA, Matthai Arquitectos. Photo by Sebastian Saldivar.)

Figure 4.5 Light and shadow on this patio blend playfully with the sculptural aspects of the brightly painted features and warm terra-cotta pottery. *(Arq. Diego Matthai, IIDA, Matthai Arquitectos. Photo by Sebastian Saldivar.)*

Figure 4.6 The use of traditional embellishments in this loft interior enhances the architectural integrity of this space. *(Braun Design, Ltd., Maura Braun, IIDA. Photo © George Lambrose, Lambrose Photography, Inc.)*

to achieve a playful look, paint the ductwork, columns, and so on in contrasting accent colors. Since loft and studio spaces are quite open, bolder colors and large-scale artwork can be used dramatically. Aside from color, another way to emphasize the mass of the space is to keep furniture to a minimum and select very streamlined pieces. The fabrics used should be of fine patterns, or no pattern at all. Leather is a very sophisticated look in a contemporary setting. Architects Ludwig Mies van der Rohe and Le Corbusier designed many well-known pieces of furniture to suit the contemporary lines of their architecture. Of course, as with any type of space, loft and studio styles can vary greatly, as demonstrated in Figures 4.7 through 4.14.

Efficient use of furniture is a key element in all small spaces, but with a studio or loft, there's the added issue of furniture placement. Many of these spaces don't have smooth, even walls that are conducive to having a lot of furniture pushed against them, so they will do better with freestanding items. If this is the case, you may need to purchase items that are finished on all sides so that unfinished backs or sides are not left exposed. (See Figures 4.15 and 4.16.)

Figure 4.7 With storage at a premium in small spaces, a storage wall that doubles as a room divider will help to balance the use of the spaces. (Designer: Lance Hosey, AIA. Photography by Robert Kassabian.)

Figure 4.8 Repetition of color, texture, and pattern add character to a living area with neutral walls and flooring. *(Braun Design, Ltd., Maura Braun, IIDA. Photo © George Lambrose, Lambrose Photography, Inc.)*

Figure 4.9 The dramatic use of black and red furnishings gives this monochromatic space style and distinction. *(Designcorp., Chris Jordan.)*

Figure 4.10   The eclectic blend of contemporary lines creates movement and an interesting flow in a typical rectilinear space. *(Andrew Liberty Interiors, IIDA.)*

Figure 4.11   This contemporary entrance relies on the use of large-scale windows and derives all of its color from nature. *(Mike Sinclair/Gould Evans.)*

Figure 4.12   This open living plan demonstrates how functional areas such as the kitchen can be blended into the space. This kitchen has been "floated" in the space without impacting the integrity of the ceiling lines or exterior windows and has become a strong design element. *(Michael Spillers/Gould Evans.)*

When considering color palettes and furnishings for your loft or studio space, it's helpful to keep the following in mind:

- If the space is irregular in shape or has many details such as exposed ductwork or walls that have several built-out areas to conceal wiring or pipes, keep the color palette to light, monochromatic colors. The furniture can be placed in groupings centered around area rugs in deeper accenting or contrasting colors.

- Pay attention to the flow of traffic throughout the space. If you're meandering through your living space rather than traveling in straighter lines, then you're likely wasting space to circulation that could be used for something else. Try to have your circulation areas perform double duty by lining a pathway with a narrow bench for seating or storage cabinets that you'll need to open only when you are storing something inside.

Figure 4.13 The colorful tile and the simplicity of these contemporary cabinets provide elegance and efficiency in this kitchen and show how space can be maximized. *(Photo by Peter Paige.)*

Figure 4.14 A long rectilinear space can be creatively and efficiently designed when it is properly planned. The effective use of the vertical area within the kitchen maximizes the storage capacity. *(Photo by Peter Paige.)*

- As you select paint colors, consider keeping window and door trim white, off-white, or metallic. The windows will seem larger than if the trim has a darker accent color. The doors will stand out less and blend into the wall area, therefore creating a cleaner, less cluttered look.

- If you have a large window that can be used as a focal point, try positioning the furniture perpendicular to the window rather than parallel in front of it to create a more spacious feel.

In Figures 4.17 and 4.18, we see a relatively open space with the kitchen and bath on one end. This type of space would work equally well as an open studio, using the office niche as a den or sleeping area. Consider multiuse furniture within the space such as bookcases or storage units that can double as room dividers, sleep sofas for sleeping or lounging, and modular furniture pieces that will allow you to change on a whim.

Bright contrasting color palettes can be a dramatic way to draw attention to one area in a loft or studio. (See Figure 4.19.)

Figure 4.15 The designer demonstrates how volume of a space can be maximized through the proper placement and efficient use of the furnishings. The earth-tone palette creates an inviting interior. *(Braun Design, Ltd., Maura Braun, IIDA. Photo © George Lambrose, Lambrose Photography, Inc.)*

Figure 4.16 This contemporary loft is a playful expression of color and form. Each function is pronounced with oversized furnishings in bold, clear colors. *(K2S Design Studio; Kathryn B. Adams and Stephanie Skovron.)*

Figure 4.17 The substantial forms with the soft seating contrast well with the expansive, brick surround window and the informal dining area. *(K2S Design Studio; Kathryn B. Adams and Stephanie Skovron.)*

Figure 4.18 This view shows an efficient home-office niche adjacent to the dining area. *(K2S Design Studio; Kathryn B. Adams and Stephanie Skovron.)*

Figure 4.19 This contemporary loft space is fun and bright. It's a creative demonstration of color blocking, where the floor is black and white, with hot pink accents throughout the room. *(Photo by Peter Paige.)*

Using an Eclectic Style in Multiuse Spaces

If your style isn't distinctly traditional or contemporary, you're likely drawn to the style known as *eclectic*. Eclectic design allows you to combine traditional and contemporary elements within the same space to create your own personal look. (See Figures 4.20 and 4.21.) A traditional space with many wonderful architectural details can be finished with contemporary palettes of color and simple contemporary furnishings, just as a contemporary space can be finished and furnished with traditional elements. If the space is open and contemporary, but you prefer traditional furnishings, then keep the finishes on the walls neutral. Another effective look is to contrast the colors of the furnishings with the colors of the space itself. This will allow the furnishings to become the focal element of the design. This is important in a small space because too many focal elements will make the space seem overwhelming and crowded. Figure 4.22 demonstrates this very effectively.

The spaces illustrated in Figures 4.23 to 4.27 use the principles of shape and form to delineate functions within their multipurpose living areas.

Figure 4.20 *Soft plums give this contemporary loft a feeling of tranquility. This space demonstrates the physiological effect that color schemes have on us. (Photo by Peter Paige.)*

Figure 4.21 Warm gold walls are enhanced by the glow of the pendant lighting. The clerestory windows give the space an open, airy feel. The use of hardwood floors with black-and-white tile make this an eclectic design. *(Photo by Peter Paige.)*

Figure 4.22 Contemporary architectural elements mixed with exquisite period furnishings create a stately feeling within this eclectic loft living/dining room. *(Photo by Peter Paige.)*

Figure 4.23 Diverse selections of furnishings, accessories, and geometric shapes are used in lieu of color by the designer to give character and expression to this eclectic space. *(K2S Design Studio; Kathryn B. Adams and Stephanie Skovron.)*

Figure 4.24 This informal kitchen and bar area shows uniformity of pattern between the unique tile selection and seating. When key accents or design elements repeat throughout a space, they lend uniformity to the design. This is especially effective with an eclectic design since many different elements may be blended in one space. *(K2S Design Studio; Kathryn B. Adams and Stephanie Skovron.)*

Figure 4.25 This view illustrates how the space lends itself to entertaining, with the soft seating adjacent to the serving and dining area. *(K2S Design Studio; Kathryn B. Adams and Stephanie Skovron.)*

Figure 4.26   Irregular ceilings are very common in loft spaces. The simple yet effective lighting approach washes the ceiling lines, which gives the space more perceived volume. A natural color palette enhances the size and scale of the interior. *(Christina Oliver. Photo © by Brian Vanden Brink.)*

Figure 4.27 *This home office within a loft space is an effective and efficient use of corner space. With square footage at a premium, it's desirable to have every niche designed for a purpose. Small corners can often be lost opportunities for fun color additions. This corner would go unnoticed without the addition of this bold color. (Photo by Peter Paige.)*

Summary

Throughout this chapter we've presented the concept of studio and loft spaces, the types of buildings they're usually found in, how to delineate different areas, and some basics for finishing and furnishing for various styles. Keep in mind that these are only suggestions. The styles and availability of studio and loft spaces vary greatly, and the styles and availability of furnishings do, too. As you define your own personal style through your living space, remember to select what you like, and don't force yourself into a particular style or look that doesn't feel right to you. The most important lesson in this chapter is to avoid overfurnishing your space. A few well-conceived pieces of furniture will help you avoid a cluttered look in your living space.

CHAPTER 5

Weekend Retreats and Guesthouses

The ultimate small space for relaxation is the weekend retreat or guesthouse. It's the place where you'll go to get away from daily life, and it should be designed with that in mind. The colors should be restful and make you and your guests feel immediately transported to a place where you feel most relaxed and can recharge.

Whether you're designing a newly built weekend retreat or renovating a guesthouse, the goal is to create a comfortable and relaxing environment. Because these spaces were not intended to be the primary living space, most retreats and guesthouses tend to be small. They may be in areas along coastlines, deep in the woods, on lakefronts, or in mountainous terrain, which can limit the size of the structure to be built. Many older guesthouses are renovated carriage houses, boathouses or servant quarters that were once part of larger estates. Today, weekend retreats are not limited to old, renovated structures. In this chapter we'll discuss the most important considerations for selecting a particular theme, how to integrate geographical location into your design, how to choose restful color palettes, and the importance of putting comfort first and foremost in your design plans. Since color will play a key role in these elements, it may be helpful to refer to Chapter 2, which discusses the psychological and physiological responses we have to different colors. In a nutshell, people feel differently in the presence of varying colors in their environments. Scientists know that we have psychological color associations and respond physiologically to both color and light. Armed with this information, we can begin to formulate our color palettes based on our own color associations. (See Figure 5.1.)

In this chapter, we'll profile the following:

- Selecting a theme

- Geographical influences

- Integrating the exterior environment with the interior design

- Selecting a restful color palette that will transport its occupants

Figure 5.1 *The combination of refined elegance and a monochromatic palette help to harmonize the dining space with the pool area. (Gauthier-Stacy, Inc. Photographer: Sam Gray.)*

tities, contrasted with pale, almost whitewashed neutrals. A big bowl of seashells or some large conch shells placed throughout the space will remind you of walks on the beach. Tropical plants like orchids, bougainvillea, hibiscus, gardenia, some ferns, and broad, glossy-leaf varieties in colorful pottery will add both color and atmosphere. Ceiling fans to gently move light, gauzy fabrics draped over windows and even walls will create an exotic ambience. Furnish with bamboo and wicker combined with dark, French-Caribbean-motif cabinets or armoires if you prefer the West Indian look. Lighting should be soft and indirect. Torchères in the corners, accent light on artwork, and pendants for task light will be sufficient. As far as lighting goes, don't forget candles and kerosene torches for added evening ambience. (See Figures 5.2 and 5.3.)

If you're timid about using too much bright color, try adding it through accents like artwork, pottery and throw pillows.

Selecting a Theme

Getting started can be the hardest part of creating your sanctuary, so you'll want to start with what you know. Perhaps you've done a lot of traveling. If not, it's likely you've read of, seen on television or in books, or simply fantasized about a place in which you'd like to spend time. With the wealth of information at your fingertips, you can create your own personal sanctuary or retreat where you can get away from the day-to-day chaos and feel relaxed. Your color palette will be reflective of the environment you're trying to create. Some suggested palettes follow.

Caribbean Themes

Use pale blue-greens, vivid coral, bright parrot green, lime green, and sunset pink in varying quan-

Figure 5.2 *Caribbean theme color palette.*

Figure 5.3 The tropical setting becomes a backdrop for this inviting living room. Designing with collectibles, diverse textures, and small amounts of color is a successful solution when an outside view becomes an important part of the interior design. *(Gauthier-Stacy, Inc. Photographer: Sam Gray.)*

African Themes

Think of Serengeti green, desert browns, rich gold hues, clay red, indigo blues, ebony black, ivory white. Set these colors in varying amounts against a backdrop of neutral brown and gold in light to medium hues. Accent with native tribal masks, costume pieces, or tools. Plants and grasses that recall the African plains, planted in shallow bowls and clustered in groupings rather than spread around too much, will contribute texture and additional green hues. Fresh exotic flowers in African vases can be added. Like the Caribbean, Africa is a hot climate, so light, airy fabrics on windows and walls painted in rich hues will also contribute to the ambience. Mosquito netting suspended over the bed would be a typical detail in Africa. The furniture would likely be dark, exotic woods that are either rustic or very refined depending on the particular locale you are trying to re-create. Upholstery fabrics may be dark, heavy tapestries, velvets, or leather, which combine beautifully with the dark woods. Wainscot on the walls can be a great way to bring rich wood tones into the space if you want to keep the furniture on the lighter scale with wicker and bamboo. Lighting can be dramatic if you highlight artwork and wash some of the focal walls with light. Candles and kerosene lamps at night will add drama. (See Figures 5.4 to 5.6.)

Engage all of the senses. Music and sound will contribute to the mood or theme you're trying to achieve, so collect tapes and CDs that will help you to connect to wherever you want to be.

Figure 5.5 This dramatic entrance displays color intensity on the wall and plays well as a backdrop to the terra-cotta plant pots and the greenery. *(Gill Smith, Interior and Landscape Designer, Auckland, New Zealand.)*

Asian Themes

Think of colors that evoke gemstones such as jade, carnelian, moonstone, opal, onyx, citrine, and turquoise; bright China red and yellow; and soft gold and brown hues of bamboo and teak. Use the brightest colors against medium to light hues of grey. The softer-intensity colors (moonstone and opal) can be used as overall background color with jade, carnelian, citrine, and turquoise as accents and accessories. Accents might include silk-screened wall hangings, rice-paper screens or partitions, tea or sake sets, and artwork or sculpture of dragons, birds, or other totems, which can be very richly detailed and colored. If the space has no room for a freestanding rice-paper screen, try incorporating

Figure 5.4 African theme color palette.

Figure 5.6 *The Southwestern theme of this home is enhanced by the interior plants and the wood furnishings. Accent pillows in rich red, gold, and plum tones add just the right touch of color to this bright, airy space. (Lori W. Carroll, ASID, IIDA. William Lesch Photography.)*

framed rice-paper panels into your window treatments. Flowers have great significance in the Asian culture and are highly revered. Beautiful bonsai trees, orchids, and bamboo trees are very accessible in most places around the world and can be planted in Asian pots. If you want soft colors, try the Japanese Blue Willow pattern or, for a bolder look, a bright lacquered red or black. Asian style combines both light and dark woods with lacquered finishes, and the furniture is very simple and straightforward. Your dining area can be a low table with floor cushions for seating, and the sleeping area will likely be a futon, either on a low, slatted platform or directly on the floor. Water fountains, rock gardens, and aquariums are also important elements in the Asian culture. Lighting will be soft and indirect. Rice-paper or silk lamps come in various shapes, colors, and sizes and are a simple way to inexpensively light most areas. If you have artwork, sculpture, plants, or a water fountain, this will be the place for accent light. (See Figures 5.7 and 5.8.)

Figure 5.7 *Asian theme color palette.*

> *Monotone color palettes calm the space and slow the pace.*

New England Themes

For this theme choose summer's nautical blues, barn reds, and grass green; autumn foliage colors of gold, orange, and russet; springtime colors of meadow green, violet, and yellow; and winter's ice blue, snow white, brown, and pussy willow grey. In New England, background colors suitable for all of the colors listed would be palettes of soft, natural hues that you would find in beach rocks and seashells, such as shades of beige, brown, grey, pink, ivory, pale yellow, and off-white. Because New England has four dramatically different seasonal changes and varying geography, you have a variety of options, and you'll want to select the palette that appeals most to you. If you want to be in the mountains, then your accents will likely be more rustic in nature. The palette will have several shades of brown and green with accents in the brighter colors of barn red, bright yellow, and blues. Wood trim and accents can have a rough-hewn look and a natural finish. If your New England retreat is on the coastline, then choose colors such as nautical blue and yellow set against sky blue, with accents of violet and red and white-washed wood accents. Again, in creating your palette, think about where you want to be and what makes you feel most relaxed. If you like the seacoast, then consider painted floors with braided area rugs and furniture like Adirondack chairs, tables, and ottomans. New England furniture has a sturdy, purposeful look. Many Shaker and Early American styles will blend nicely into these themes. Because of the salty air and moisture, many pieces were painted for outdoor use. Bird feeders and wind chimes enhance the sound ambience. Indoor plants are important, but don't forget window boxes, planted with seasonal foliage. Typ-

Figure 5.8 This charming tropical retreat illustrates how using color for interest and contrast can create energy within a space. The wood ceiling and the blue-and-white pattern on the furniture balance the room. *(Photo by Peter Paige.)*

ical plantings include impatiens in soft colors, geranium with bursts of bright color, mums in soft to rich earth tones, lilacs, roses, forsythia, and various evergreen foliage. The plantings you select will be determined by your own personal likes and dislikes and by whatever is indigenous to your retreat. Lighting is tricky in New England due to the shortness of available daylight during some times of the year. For the purposes of creating a retreat, we suggest a moderate amount of overall light from recessed and surface-applied light fixtures, and add task light through pendants and floor or table lamps. Lampshades can be of stained glass or oilpaper styles. Nautical wall sconces (also known as *bulkhead fixtures*) are good utilitarian light. They come in white, brass, bronze, and black and can be applied to a wall or ceiling, indoors or out. For added charm, light kerosene lamps with colored glass covers of amber, green, blue, or red in the evening, or votive lights in sea glass colors. (See Figures 5.9 to 5.12.)

Remember, these are only suggestions. You may have visited particular places in Africa, Asia, New England, or the Caribbean that differ from these palettes. It will be your own color associations that you'll need to follow to create a space that's right for you.

Figure 5.9 New England theme color palette.

Figure 5.10 The stone fireplace anchors this warm retreat, and it becomes the focal point for the entire space. The monochromatic scheme balances the natural finishes used throughout the interior. The natural finishes and upholstery add textural variety to the room. The only accent colors are found in accessories, artwork, and the floral arrangement. *(Christina Oliver. Brian VandenBrink, Photographer © 2002.)*

Figure 5.11   This playful coastal design gives this room scale with the use of navy blue on the ceiling and on a portion of the wall. The area rug and throw pillows help to balance the dramatic striped-pattern wall covering, while the sheer drapery fabric lightens and softens the otherwise bold interior space. *(Mark Woodman, CMG.)*

Figure 5.12 Colorful pottery stools and a coordinating table base demonstrate a creative design solution for an informal gathering area. The matching floral arrangement and window treatment balance the space and frame the outside view. *(K2S Design Studio, Kathryn B. Adams and Stephanie Skovron.)*

Geographical Influences

The geographical location of your weekend retreat or guesthouse will influence your design theme. Let's say your retreat is in the Arizona mountains and the theme you want to create is distinctly Asian. You may be able to include Asian embellishments such as furniture, but when you look out the window, you're going to see red rock—not a misty landscape. Geographically, it makes sense to align the theme of your retreat space more closely with the indigenous climate. Unless you have a very clear picture of a theme that you want to re-create, we recommend looking at the geography and climate in which the guesthouse or retreat is located and work from there.

Climate is a geographical influence that will affect your color palette selection. If the space is located in a cold region, select a theme with a warm color palette; conversely, if the space is in a warm climate, select a theme that offers a cooler color palette for comfort and balance. (See Figures 5.13 and 5.14.)

Figure 5.13 The depth of the wall color combined with the mural on the armoire creates dimension, giving the room scale and balancing the space. The contrasting white staircase adds an elegant touch. *(Photo by Peter Paige.)*

Figure 5.14 *One could sit for hours enjoying the splendor and tranquility of this view. The view becomes the art in the room by turning the chair. (Photo by Peter Paige.)*

Integrating the Exterior Environment with the Interior Design

If your retreat or guesthouse has a stunning view, patio, pool, or deck, it can become an integral part of your design. A view can become the focal point just as a piece of artwork would. Let's say you have a seating arrangement near a window, position the furniture as you would to view a large piece of art-work, with the seating grouped to look at the view. A deck or patio can be nicely integrated by providing large access doors between the inside and out-side. If the patio has tile, select a style that you can also have inside the house so that your design is consistent inside and out. Here are some other suggestions:

- Limit window treatments to only what's necessary for extreme sun or protection from the cold.

- Select color palettes that are similar to the room you will enter when you walk through the door. If the room is painted a deep-hued yellow with white trim, then use the yellow outside and accent it with even deeper hues of yellow and an additional accent color or two such as turquoise and orange.

- If you have a pool area, placing a water fountain inside will create a sensory connection to the pool outside.

- If you have a patio, deck, or walking garden, install enough lighting outside so that you can enjoy the inside or outside equally well—weather permitting, of course.

- Install speakers from your sound system outside for entertaining or just relaxing.

It really makes sense to optimize any outside space you have with finishing touches that will make it more inviting to you and your guests. When dealing with a small space, make every inch count! (See Figure 5.15.)

Selecting a Restful Color Palette

When designing a space for a weekend retreat or guesthouse, you'll want to make the interior as relaxing and inviting as possible. Selecting restful colors and tones will help you to achieve that goal. Here are some suggestions:

- *Colors for tranquility.* Soft hues of blue, indigo, blue-greens, and soft greens, alone or paired with soft hues of yellow and apricot. Trim can be white, off-white, or any of the colors listed in their palest hue. (See Figure 5.16.)

Figure 5.15 The shutters, when open, allow this sitting area to feel connected to the pool area. The blue-and-white chair seems to blend into the backdrop of this oasis. *(Photo by Peter Paige.)*

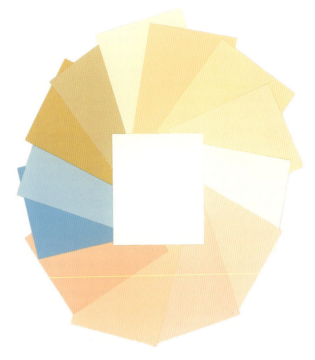

Figure 5.17 *Color palette for nurturing.*

Figure 5.16 *Color palette for tranquility.*

- *Colors for nurturing.* Pale apricot and chamois yellow with cream-colored trim. Limit accents to soft robin's egg blue or darker hues of the apricot and chamois. Trim can be white, natural wood colors, or the palest tone of any of these colors listed. (See Figure 5.17.)

- *Colors for rest and renewal.* Soft hues of seafoam green, indigo blue, and warm beige, with cream-colored trim. (See Figure 5.18.) These groupings clearly represent most of the colors you'd find while walking a beach. They're the colors of the sky, ocean, sand, and seashells. Most of us will readily admit that we feel more tranquil, nurtured, and renewed when we're relaxing on a peaceful beach. Figures 5.19 and 5.20 present some good examples of restful and relaxing color palettes.

Figure 5.18 *Color palette for rest and renewal.*

Figure 5.19 This oasis retreat is an ideal spot for relaxing, conversing, or meditating. The use of natural materials and furnishings are Zen-like. Limiting color and using organic materials can give a space a soothing appeal. The only color here is the greenery, which is very subtle. (Braun Design Ltd., Maura Braun, IIDA. Photo © George Lambrose, Lambrose Photography, Inc.)

Lighting for Your Retreat or Guesthouse

As indicated under "Selecting a Theme," lighting is an important component in creating the right atmosphere for your getaway. When selecting your lighting sources, keep the following general rules in mind:

- In task areas such as kitchen food-prep counters, bathroom mirrors, and reading chairs or game tables, provide good-quality, uniform light. Fixtures can include pendants with incandescent or low-voltage halogen bulbs, surface-mounted fixtures with incandescent bulbs and glass covers, and recessed-can downlights fitted with halogen bulbs. These are task areas where the light level needs to be of good quality, but don't overdo the intensity. A 60- or 75-watt bulb can do the job of a 100-watt bulb in most cases.

- For general overall lighting, the remaining sources should all be indirect. This can be achieved by placing torchères (floor lamps that send light up toward the ceiling) near corners and locating wall sconces in circulation areas. Additional light can be added with recessed downlights if needed, but use them only to light artwork and wash light onto walls.

- If you have an outside area such as a deck, patio, pool area, or garden, light that, too. Exterior light-

Figure 5.20 The wood furniture and flooring soften the space and balance the monotone palette of the light, sheer draperies, and linens. The wall color blends into the sheer fabric on the windows to create a relaxing and calming bedroom. *(Gauthier-Stacy, Inc. Photographer: Greg Premru.)*

ing allows guests the freedom to wander in and out and provides more-usable square footage. Exterior-rated wall sconces, post lights, and simple strings of tree lights can create a magical atmosphere at nighttime.

- Wire all of your light fixtures with dimming controls so you can adjust light level as needed.

- Nighttime lighting can be as simple as placing all of your fixtures on low dimmer or lighting candles or kerosene lamps and stringing tree lights around an entertaining area. Depending on where the guesthouse is, moonlight will be the only additional light you may need on clear nights.

Summary

As you spend time creating a private sanctuary, remember to be patient. It can take time to develop a clear vision of how you want your oasis to feel and function. Start with soft palettes of color and then slowly add to it as you discover your own likes and dislikes. You can always repaint a wall or two if you discover you like stronger hues. If your lights are on dimmers, you can turn them down if they're too bright. Relax into the process. After all, this is your sanctuary, isn't it?

PART 3

Room by Room

CHAPTER 6
Entrances and Living Rooms

As humans, first impressions are the longest lasting. With your entrance, you have the unique opportunity to set the stage for how the rest of your home presents itself. Careful consideration for the architectural style, color palettes, finishes, and furnishings will be the catalyst for how the rest of the space evolves as a whole. It's a transitional space where you shift gears from public space to private sanctuary. The lighting should be appropriate, and the use of colors, patterns, and textures should hint at what's to come beyond the threshold. Think about what sort of welcome you want for yourself and your guests.

Typically, living rooms, family rooms, or kitchens are adjacent to entrances. It's best to plan your color palettes so they flow well from the entrance into these spaces. These are rooms for conversation with family and friends, preparing meals, watching television, or relaxing at the end of a busy day.

The color palettes you choose will build the overall foundation for the final result you want to achieve, so they should flow smoothly and work well together. This chapter will review options for designing these key areas. We'll detail various styles of entrances and living rooms, outlining options to help you set the theme for these spaces within your home. (See Figure 6.1.)

Some Style Options for Entrances and Living Rooms

Whatever your style preferences, you'll want to consider the existing design features in your entrance and living room. The various styles are discussed in detail in the following sections to help you make your selections and decisions with a goal in mind. A primary goal of designing the entry as a transition space is to maintain a sense of uniformity, which will contribute to the overall concept of making the space seem larger.

For a small entry, it's important to establish a color palette that coordinates with the other rooms. This will bring unity to the area as a whole.

Figure 6.1 *The entrance area is where you create a first impression. The walls will effectively create the backdrop to the setting if you use a dramatic wall covering or mural. This artistic wall painting adds depth and drama that can't be achieved with a single paint alone. By adding depth to this small space, the entrance has a sense of scale. (Jane Considine Decorative Painting.)*

Traditional/Historical Entrances and Living Rooms

In traditional or historical spaces, the entrance was typically a transitional area to the other living spaces. Entrances and living rooms that are traditional in style are generally more formal in terms of their interior finishes, furnishings, and architectural elements. Simple palettes of warm and neutral color can be enhanced with subtle accent colors on furnishings and accessories. Figures 6.2 through 6.6 illustrate these traditional and historical room features.

Color contrasts in traditional small spaces should maintain a minimal number of accent colors. Overdoing accent colors can create an unbalanced feeling within a small living space.

When designing a traditional space using furniture as a focal point, it's important to use accent colors and patterns that are traditional or historical. For example, if you're using green, choose a hunter green as opposed to the more contemporary lime green.

Contemporary Entrances and Living Rooms

As with traditional spaces, entrances in contemporary homes should be designed as transitional areas to the other rooms. Contemporary entrances and living rooms tend to have clean lines, simple architectural details and furnishings. Color palettes can be neutral and understated, with bright or bold accent colors used through furnishings, area rugs,

Figure 6.2   This formal entry has clean, traditional lines and simple details. As in many traditional homes, the entry is also a transitional space to other living areas. *(Braun Design, LTD., Maura Braun, IIDA. Photo © George Lambrose, Lambrose Photography, Inc.)*

Figure 6.3 In this Federal-style sitting area, the soft, warm palette of traditional colors is well executed through pattern and the use of accents, thus demonstrating how to effectively add energy to a color palette that is warm and neutral. This is achieved with the use of multiple patterns and accents in the room. This works for a small space because it adds interest where the room finishes themselves are based on a neutral palette. *(Gauthier-Stacy, Inc. Photographer: Sam Gray.)*

Figure 6.4 This formal living room uses simple color contrasts to create versatility with the traditional furnishings. *(Bennett Phillips, Phillips Design Resources.)*

Figure 6.5   This traditional sitting area incorporates some contemporary furnishings to allow the owner's personality to emerge. Note that the color palette of the space is neutral with contrasting dark wood, while the upholstery on the furnishings is of a warm, soft-hued complementary palette. *(Bennett Phillips, Phillips Design Resources.)*

Figure 6.6   This is a fine example of how simple color palettes allow the furnishings to become the focal point of the space. *(Andrew Liberty, Interiors, IIDA.)*

accessories, and artwork which then become the details of the space. The design approach of using neutral finishes is to give you more long-term flexibility—you won't have to repaint the entire space to change the look. Accent lighting, such as sconces or wall washers, will nicely embellish an entrance, accent a wall, or highlight a piece of artwork. The lighting should be soft enough so the space feels warm and welcoming, not harsh or bright. When greeting guests, adjust the light levels so the entertaining areas are slightly brighter than the entry area to visually enhance the transitional quality of the entry space. If all of your lights are wired with dimming switches, this can easily be done. (See Chapter 3 for an in-depth discussion of lighting). Figures 6.7 through 6.10 illustrate features of contemporary entrances and living rooms.

Figure 6.7 In this contemporary loft apartment, the space itself becomes art because of its sculptural quality. The painting adds color and warmth by enhancing the wood tones in the handrail and floor material. *(Braun Design, LTD., Maura Braun, IIDA. Photo © George Lambrose, Lambrose Photography, Inc.)*

Figure 6.8 The creative use of light and warm accent colors balance well with the strong contemporary motif of this living space. *(Tom Gass, IIDA, Gass Design. Photographer: Peter Paige.)*

Figure 6.9 The clean lines of the contemporary furnishings give this traditional home a classic, elegant feel. (*Gauthier-Stacy, Inc. Photographer: Greg Premlu.*)

Figure 6.10 The simple addition of lacquered accents gives this contemporary living space an exotic, Asian feel. (*Andrew Liberty Interiors, IIDA.*)

Formal or Opulent Entrances and Living Rooms

Elegant and classic detailing such as crown and picture molding, chair rails and wainscot, coffered ceilings, and multilayers of patterns and fabric treatments are all attributes for formal or opulent entrances and living rooms. The function of an opulent living room is typically formal, including fea-tures such as a well-balanced seating area and added attention to detail through window treat-ments, accessories, and lighting. Furnishings with clean lines, used with a warm, off-white palette would give a classic feeling to a small living room. Figures 6.11 through 6.13 are examples of entrances and living rooms with a formal and opulent appeal.

Figure 6.11 When entering a small space it's a good idea to use every possible opportunity for extra seating. This formal entry serves more than one function by introducing a balanced seating arrangement. *(Gauthier-Stacy, Inc. Photographer: Sam Gray.)*

Figure 6.12 This cozy sitting area becomes formal through the use of neutral tones and tailored lines of the furnishings. The simple, classic accent details add an opulent touch. Note the height of the drapery hardware makes the most of the window opening and creates a beautiful long vertical ine. *(Gauthier-Stacy, Inc. Photographer: Sam Gray.)*

Figure 6.13 The fine wood detailing and richly appointed furnishings against a warm, off-white backdrop lend an air of opulence to this space. *(Chris Jordan, Designcorp.)*

Figure 6.14 This area shows that an entry can be small and still have impact. The geometry of the space creates interest by directing the occupant around the entire space rather than through the rooms. The soft, natural palette is nicely accented with rich textural elements and depth of color in the metals, area rug, and wood. *(Lori W. Carroll, ASID, IIDA. William Lesch Photography.)*

Eclectic Entrances and Living Rooms

An eclectic design for entrances and living rooms is created when various periods and styles are used in concert within the same space. (See Figures 6.14 to 6.20.) This occurs most commonly when our personal style contrasts with the inherent architectural style, and it is an especially difficult theme to work with in a small space. If the space is contemporary and you are fond of traditional furnishings, then select one or two colors that coordinate with most of your furniture and use that for your background, or

Figure 6.15 *This is the immediate view on entering this home. In lieu of having a separate entry space, the designer created openness to the adjacent space. The open shelves and ornament create the needed separation, and the guests get a glimpse of what the evening has in store. Also note the finishes are very organic, which creates a subtle transition. (Lori W. Carroll, ASID, IIDA. William Lesch Photography.)*

Figure 6.16 *The fireplace and architectural elements of this room blend with the contemporary furniture, lighting, and finishes to create an eclectic appeal. (Photo by Peter Paige.)*

Figure 6.17 This cool woodland retreat owes its success to the warm, organic textures in the carpet and furniture. The organic color palette integrates the exterior environment with the living space and gives the impression that the space is larger than it actually is. (Christina Oliver. Brian Vanden Brink, Photographer, © 2002.)

base colors. Conversely, if the space is traditional in nature, and you prefer contemporary furnishings, then try neutrals or off-white for the background color. Vary the finish of the colors with glossy trim and matte walls in the same color. This also applies to a space that is nonspecific in style.

It's important to create subtle transitions in a small space. Soft, organic earth tones will achieve this by creating a sense of continuity from room to room.

Figure 6.18 The cool paint color balances well with the soft, organic furnishings and accents to create an interesting eclectic theme. *(Mark Woodman, CMG.)*

Figure 6.19   As with many traditional spaces, the use of a neutral color palette for both walls and trim will diminish the busyness of the backdrop and allow the details to come forward. Notice that the built-ins, stained-glass window, and the antique furnishings are the focal point, not the walls and trim. This design strategy works well in small spaces, as the room appears larger by maintaining a neutral palette on both the walls and trim. *(Treena Crochet, A Matter of Style, LTD. Photo © Stephen SetteDucati.)*

Figure 6.20   This eclectic living room combines rich wood tones, geometric shapes, and vivid colors to create a warm, inviting space that highlights the original artwork displayed. *(Arq. Diego Matthai, IIDA, Matthai Arquitectos. Photo by Sebastian Saldivar.)*

Tropical Entrances and Living Rooms

Tropical themes are designed with colors, furnishings, accessories, and plantings found in warm climates. Floors and walls are usually simple and neutral in color; however, the goal here is to create spaces that have an exotic feel. This can be achieved through textured walls, dark exotic woods, and cultural accessories. Figures 6.21 through 6.24 are wonderful illustrations of this unique style.

Practical Considerations for Entrances and Living Rooms

As with any other living space, there are various components that need to be considered during the planning stages of your entrance and living rooms. There will be overall layout and design issues, potential structural considerations, floor and wall materials and finishes, and lighting design. Depending on the complexity, you will also need to deter-

Figure 6.21   The arid climate is evident in the desert-type plantings bordering this entry area and in the simple, warm colors used on the walls and in the planters. *(Gill Smith Interior and Landscape Designer, Auckland, New Zealand.)*

Figure 6.22 Light, cool tones combined with rich, dark woods are contrasts often used in warm, tropical climates. Dark woods are typical of the more exotic species, which are found in tropical climates. Light-colored palettes are often used in warmer climates to give a cool, airy feeling to a room. The accessories and plantings further enhance this theme. *(Gauthier-Stacy, Inc. Photographer: Sam Gray.)*

Figure 6.23 This waterside lounge area is cool and inviting, largely due to the light furnishings, simple accents, and tropical plantings. *(Gauthier-Stacy, Inc. Photographer: Sam Gray.)*

Figure 6.24 Although the floor and walls of this living space are simple and neutral, the space feels rich and exotic because of the deep accent wall, warm earth-toned furniture, and cultural accessories. *(Lori W. Carroll, ASID, IIDA. William Lesch Photography.)*

mine whether this is a job you can do alone or whether you will need the assistance of a skilled designer, architect, or contractor. Added issues you'll want to think about include the following:

- How much daily use will these spaces get?

- Do I want to entertain often?

- What are my storage needs? (This includes built-ins for books, games, media equipment, television, and general display shelves.)

- Will my living room be used for watching television, reading, entertaining, or all three? (This will affect the durability of finish materials and storage needs.)

- What are my lighting and electrical needs?

The appendix, "Guidelines for Getting Started," offers additional help in deciding whether to work with a contractor or to take on the project yourself.

Summary

This chapter has demonstrated the importance of establishing the entrance and living room as the foundation for the rest of the rooms in your home. It will be your choice whether to design them to build up to a focal point in another room or to make the entrance or living room play that part. Chapter 7 will explore a similar variety of options for kitchens that may well become the focal point to which the entrance and living room transition.

CHAPTER 7

Kitchens and Dining Rooms

The kitchen is the heart of a home, and it tends to function as a gathering area for most families. The challenge with small spaces is how to blend efficiency for the cook(s) with room for gathering. Just as the entrance serves as a transitional space into a living room, the kitchen design and color palettes will likely be transitional into your dining room, and you'll want to coordinate designs for both areas together. In this chapter, we'll identify several style options for kitchens and dining rooms and offer illustrations from designers around the world. For detailed information on material and lighting selection, refer to Chapter 3.

Some Style Options for Kitchens and Dining Rooms

As you begin to plan the design for your kitchen and dining room, look at the interaction between the spaces. Many will naturally flow into one another while some will not. The following sections present some of the various approaches to kitchen and dining areas and practical considerations for each.

Traditional/Historical Kitchens and Dining Rooms

Historically, kitchens were not necessarily the "heart of the home." They were often extensions of the main house, where meals were prepared and cooked in enormous fireplaces or on woodburning stoves. Meals were then served in the formal dining room, which was separate. As time passed, kitchens evolved to include room for eating and gathering, thus becoming the center of activity. The rooms weren't always efficient because of the changes caused by adding modern conveniences over the years. Things like central heating and plumbing often added many cumbersome details around which to design, although few homes remain that present this specific issue. Most kitchens and dining areas in today's traditional and historical homes already have central heat and plumbing, but if any of these reminders of the past remain, they can be used to enhance your overall design. These features often include unique niches, high ceilings, wood floors, wainscot, and sometimes fireplaces. To maximize storage and create the feeling of a larger space, build or place cabinets in niche areas, or bring them all the way to the ceiling, taking advantage of as much vertical storage capacity as possible.

The uniqueness of traditional and historical kitchens has been in their practical approach to having different areas for different tasks and with that, various counter and cabinet heights to address each need. Areas were efficient, but the overall kitchen was not. With a small kitchen area, if your goal is a traditional or historical look, then select one area you want to highlight and make that distinctive. It may be a baking center where you replicate an old Hoosier, the cooking area, or the sink. Many sink manufacturers offer traditional soapstone designs, which can be a beautiful addition. Soapstone was commonly used because of its ability to retain heat, thus maintaining warm enough water in the sink for dishwashing. Whatever area you select, the rest of the kitchen will need to be as efficient as possible, with facilities for preparing, washing, and cooking in appropriate adjacencies to your cooking needs. This is often referred to as the *work triangle,* and the objective is to have the distances be as equal as possible.

Floors were often wood, mosaic tile, or linoleum tile, many walls had wainscot in painted and natural wood finishes, sometimes extending several feet up the wall, and ceilings with tin panels could be found. Typical counter and backsplash materials were oiled soapstone, slate, wood, marble, and even linoleum. For an authentic look in today's small kitchens, wood floors with colorful scatter rugs or patterned linoleum or vinyl tile work well. Counters of oiled soapstone, slate, and granite will look best, but plastic laminate in a style that mimics the older finishes can also be used. Backsplashes of coordinating tile, especially mosaic sizes, add practical charm. Paint colors can be anything from white to medium tones, but try to find a common color that works with all of your furnishings and keep it simple. Accessories can add the needed finishing details and make it uniquely yours. Try hanging herb bundles or pot racks with wrought iron finish to display copper and iron cooking pans. the accessory options are limit-

less, but try to select items that are representative of the period you are trying to re-create.

A traditional or historical dining room should have a classic, elegant ambience. Using an appropriate color palette, wall and window treatments, or period furnishings in your dining room can achieve a traditional, elegant look. There are many historical and traditional paint colors available on the market to help you plan your color schemes for the image you desire. Deep tones of burgundy, hunter green, navy blue, and rich gold are often used. (Figure 7.1 is a good example of a traditional color palette.) A wide variety of wall-covering styles and patterns for traditional or historical dining rooms are also available, including damask, toile, and traditional prints or

Figure 7.1 The warm, rich traditional color palette of this efficient kitchen and breakfast bar creates a cozy retreat. *(Photograph and Design by Susan Stowell for Interior Solutions.)*

stripes. When selecting your wall covering or finish, look at your existing space elements. Architectural details, existing floor finishes, and your existing furnishings may be determining factors for your choice of traditional or historical wall treatment. With limited space, the seating capacity for entertaining also needs to be considered. A good example of appropri-ate seating for a traditional dining room in a small space would be a drop-leaf table that can be pushed against a wall when not in use. Also, a small niche area could have a table with extension leafs to give an expandable option (for temporary use) when guests are over for dinner. Figures 7.1 through 7.5 demonstrate several of these treatments.

Figure 7.2 The interesting niches available in many traditional and historical homes are used beautifully in this kitchen with this antique storage cabinet. The simple whitewashed beadboard walls and table, paired with the wood floor, is a fine example of how to keep it simple. *(Treena Crochet, A Matter of Style, Ltd. Photo © Stephen SetteDucati.)*

Figure 7.3 This traditional home shows how the kitchen can be efficiently designed with a small amount of space. The designer has taken advantage of the high ceilings by creating cabinetry that goes directly to the ceiling. The warm terra-cotta floors and area rug balance the light finish of the cabinet. (*Braun Design, Ltd., Maura Braun, IIDA. Photo © George Lambrose, Lambrose Photography, Inc.*)

Figure 7.4 This traditional dining room starts with warm white walls, trim, and ceiling, rich dark wood trim, plank flooring, and an elegant marble fireplace mantle. The designer has then carried through simple wood finishes, layered traditional fabrics, and several traditional accents in the furnishings. *(Bennett Phillips, Phillips Design Resources.)*

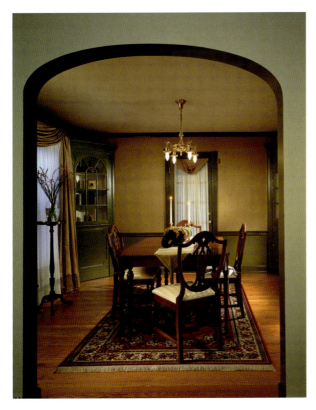

Figure 7.5 Two tones of traditional color give this dining room a casual, classic elegance. The Oriental carpet adds complementary color. *(Braun Design, Ltd., Maura Braun, IIDA. Photo © George Lambrose, Lambrose Photography, Inc.)*

Contemporary Kitchens and Dining Rooms

In selecting color palettes for small contemporary kitchens and dining rooms, monochromatic and monotone color palettes in warm tones are good choices. These palettes create the feeling of openness, which is ideal for small spaces. Some contemporary styles use added color to create a focal point for added interest. This can be done with decorative tile in a countertop or backsplash, or in a brightly-colored piece of artwork on an end wall. The neutral colors in monotone palettes are conducive to minimalist design, which also works well in small spaces. Figures 7.6 through 7.10 are excellent examples of how to create an effective contemporary design using these principles.

Formal/Opulent Kitchens and Dining Rooms

Formal or opulent kitchens and dining rooms are practical if the style of your interior space is in line with this type of image. For instance, if your space has a simple, minimalist feeling, with few (if any) architectural embellishments, a formal or opulent design could not be easily achieved. If your space is traditional or historical, however, it would have some relevance to a formal style.

Be careful not to overwhelm a small space with too much opulence. Use large-scale or ornate furnishings sparingly, and use fabrics in moderation.

Figure 7.6   *This minimalist dining room blends wood, metal, and stone to create a dynamic space. Color becomes a focal point. (Arq. Diego Matthai, IIDA, Matthai Arquitectos. Photo by Sebastian Saldivar.)*

Figure 7.7 The sleek lines and geometry of this kitchen make a cheerful, efficient workspace. The opening wall allows friends to converse without needing to disrupt the cook's process. The color palette is neutral, but warm. *(Tom Gass, IIDA, Gass Design. Photographer: Peter Paige.)*

Figure 7.8 This dining room is a fine example of minimalist design. Note the texture in the carpet and how it contrasts with the sleek lines in the wood finish. *(Braun Design, Ltd., Maura Braun, IIDA. Photo © George Lambrose, Lambrose Photography, Inc.)*

Figure 7.9 Contemporary style is at its best when done with monotone palettes. This dining space becomes opulent through the rich appointment of accessories and the depth of the wood tone in the table. *(Braun Design, Ltd., Maura Braun, IIDA. Photo © George Lambrose, Lambrose Photography, Inc.)*

Figure 7.10 Muted earth tones combine with smooth textures to establish this contemporary living room and accentuate the artwork. *(Arq. Diego Matthai, IIDA, Matthai Arquitectos. Photo by Sebastian Saldivar.)*

While opulent color palettes are often neutral, rich jewel tones could add a sense of drama to your dining-room setting and will create an intimate dining experience. Figures 7.11 through 7.15 demonstrate elegant executions of an opulent style. A good example of an opulent wall treatment is the use of toile wallpaper in Figure 7.14. Suggested upholstery fabrics are damasks or silks, and window treatments would cascade or puddle to the floor.

Figure 7.11 Drama and elegance are the signatures for this opulent dining room. The color palette is warm, deep, and complementary. (Photo by Peter Paige.)

Figure 7.12 The floor and walls are light and neutral colors, while the cabinetry glows with a rich wood tone, creating opulent dining space. (Lori W. Carroll, ASID, IIDA. William Lesch Photography.)

Figure 7.13 The simplicity of this room, typical in many small spaces, allows the furnishings to be the focal point. *(Michele F. Toto, Assoc. IIDA & IDS. Photographer: Mary Wynn-Ball, Wynn Ball Studios, New York.)*

Figure 7.14 Everything about this space is warm and opulent. The toile wallpaper adds depth and character, while the simple raw silk window-dressing fabric adds elegance. The furniture is an eclectic blend of antique Hepplewhite. It's all brought together with the well-dressed table and crystal chandelier. *(Gauthier-Stacy, Inc. Photographer: Sam Gray.)*

Figure 7.15 The dark wood cabinets and countertops visually ground the space to create a more intimate scale. *(Lori W. Carroll, ASID, IIDA. William Lesch Photography.)*

Eclectic Kitchens and Dining Rooms

Kitchens and dining rooms become eclectic designs when one or more periods or styles are combined. Traditional accessories or accents in a dining room with a contemporary design would be an example of a space with eclectic qualities. Figures 7.16 through 7.20 illustrate how to blend styles for an eclectic look in a kitchen or dining room. Figure 7.18 illustrates a creative use of primary colors with polished surfaces—features that are usually associated with contemporary design—in a traditional-style kitchen.

Northeastern Kitchens and Dining Rooms

Northeastern-style kitchens and dining rooms are frequently traditional, historical, or rustic in design. The use of warm color palettes, wood cabinetry, painted and stenciled finishes, and wood furnishings are quite common in this region. Figures 7.21 and 7.22 show how diverse the application of these traits can be and still remain totally appropriate for their particular environment.

Figure 7.16   This contemporary dining space becomes eclectic with the addition of formal and traditional accents. The accessories add warmth, depth, and texture. *(Tom Gass, IIDA, Gass Design. Photographer: Peter Paige.)*

Figure 7.17 This view of the same dining space shown in Figure 7.17 further illustrates how artwork and accessories bring warmth and energy into a simple, contemporary space. *(Tom Gass, IIDA, Gass Design. Photographer: Peter Paige.)*

Figure 7.18 The bright primary colors and highly polished surfaces of this kitchen demonstrate one way to energize a traditional space. This is a kitchen that anyone would love to spend time in. *(From www.tobeydesigngroup.com.)*

Figure 7.19 The striking contrast of black and white provides a strong design statement for this dining room. Again, blending of styles establishes an eclectic approach to design. *(Andrew Liberty Interiors, IIDA.)*

Figure 7.20 This blend of contemporary and neoclassical elements has become living artwork. *(Braun Design, Ltd., Maura Braun, IIDA. Photo © George Lambrose, Lambrose Photography, Inc.)*

Figure 7.21 This kitchen is very typical of Northeastern style, where traditional, historical, and industrial buildings have been renovated for living space. The colors blend warm tones, which help to counter the effects of the cold winter months. *(Bennett Phillips, Phillips Design Resources.)*

Figure 7.22 While this kitchen space is well appointed and classically styled, it takes its design cues from its environment. The rustic, woodsy charm is evident in the organic materials used throughout. *(Christina Oliver. Brian Vanden Brink, Photographer, © 2002.)*

Southern Kitchens and Dining Rooms

Southern kitchens and dining rooms often are designed using cool, light colors. Specifically, Southwestern areas, in contrast, will use rich, warmly textured color palettes, which emulate the surrounding environment. Usually, homes in southern regions have stucco or adobe construction, giving texture to the wall and ceiling finishes. Kitchen cabinets in southern climates are often raised-panel designs with whitewashed, light hardwoods or light colors of laminate finish. Southwestern cabinetry may be darker varieties of wood, painted finishes, or plastic laminate. Figures 7.23 through 7.26 demonstrate how the design in these kitchens and dining rooms relates to their specific geographical regions.

Practical Considerations for Kitchens and Dining Rooms

When faced with designing a kitchen, begin with a checklist of needs and then prioritize: Will there be any structural changes to open up a wall or relocate a major appliance or plumbing? Will my floor finish be the same in the kitchen and dining area? Is the dining room a separate area altogether? How many cooks will likely be in the kitchen at the same time?

Figure 7.23 The rich, warm colors in this palette would give the occupant the feel of being in a Southwestern climate, with or without the furnishings and accents. (Mark Woodson, CMG.)

Figure 7.24 The combination of rich color and bold texture combine to give this dining and kitchen space a Southwest feel. *(Lori W. Carroll, ASID, IIDA. William Lesch Photography.)*

Figure 7.25 and Figure 7.26 *The high ceilings and cool, light colors hint that these homes are located in a warm climate. (Carole Harrison, Auckland Kitchens.)*

How many people would I like to seat in the dining area? What are my overall storage needs for these spaces? Will I need new appliances, and, if so, what is my budget? What style of cabinetry, countertops, and backsplash do I prefer? What is my overall budget?

Before you prioritize your list, it may be helpful to meet with a kitchen contractor to assist you in determining initial costs for each facet of the work.

If budget is a consideration, make the most of small details. A good example of this would be to use a neutral floor tile and a more decorative tile on the backsplash, where it is closer to eye level and can be better appreciated. The accent tile can also be one or several highly stylized or custom tiles placed strate-

Figure 7.27 *The use of stone for both the counter and backsplash is a practical and elegant way to finish the kitchen. Stone is a classic, timeless, and practical material for kitchen design. Stone is likely to be heat- and scratch-resistant, and it's relatively easy to maintain overall. (Braun Design, Ltd., Maura Braun, IIDA. Photo © George Lambrose, Lambrose Photography, Inc.)*

Figure 7.28 *The intricate tile work in this cooking area adds depth and dimension to this kitchen and gives it a strong European character. Tile is a way to creatively add accent color to a small kitchen. (Maria P. Perron, Village House Interiors, LLC. Bill Fish Photography, Manchester, New Hampshire.)*

gically as focal points. The same can be done on the countertops. Another interesting detail that is also practical is to provide accent lighting over the main food-preparation area or dining area. The light itself can be the accent, or you might try using a tiny, low-voltage pendant to add distinction to your style. The following sections detail more practical considerations that will make planning your kitchen a positive experience. (See Figures 7.27 to 7.30.)

Cabinetry for Kitchens

The type of cabinetry you select will depend on the existing style of your home (traditional versus contemporary, for example) and on the amount and type of storage space your small-scale kitchen allows. In a small space, you'll want to maximize

Figure 7.29 *This colorful, whimsical kitchen is practical, efficient, and fun. It's been designed to allow the occupants to display colorful artwork as part of the design. (Diana Bennett-Wirtz, ASID, Amethyst Design.)*

Figure 7.30 *This is a closer view of the detail used in the whimsical kitchen shown in Figure 7.29. (Diana Bennett-Wirtz, ASID, Amethyst Design.)*

your storage capacity. The adjacencies of your appliances should also be part of the cabinetry design process. Table 7.1 lists a few of the types of cabinets available and price ranges (low, middle, or high). Figures 7.31 through 7.35 illustrate variations in cabinet types.

Countertops for Kitchens

When selecting countertop material options, heights, and function, layout requirements (e.g., sink and stovetop placement) are important elements to consider. Ease of cleaning is a very important feature to take into account, as are performance and maintenance. Table 7.2 defines the common types of mate-

Table 7.1   *General Cabinet Options*

CABINET STYLE	PRICE RANGE
Stock or premanufactured low-pressure laminates, melamine surfaces. Finishes use economy-grade wood. Construction often uses butt or rabbet joints. Hardware designed for minimal stress and loads (50 to 75 lb. applied horizontally). Door and drawer pulls are either integral to door and drawer fronts or limited in selection. Colors are limited to basic, neutral colors.	Low
Combination of stock, premanufactured cabinets with a limited number of custom sizes available. Finishes are high-pressure laminates, lacquered wood, high-density fiberboard (HDF), and wood. Custom-grade wood, with thicker surfaces than those of economy-grade cabinetry. Joinery is often mortise and tenon and lock joints. Finishes vary from whitewashed or stained to painted or varnished. Styles range from plain-front to raised-profile design. Hardware is of moderate quality (75 to 100 lb. applied horizontally), with options for alignment and full extensions in doors and drawers. Finish hardware has many options that will directly affect cost.	Middle
Custom-designed millwork cabinets in unlimited style and options. Finishes use premium-grade wood faces and are generally quartersawn hardwoods with solid construction methods (e.g., full box drawers, matched grain patterns, mitered corners, dowels, and dovetail joints). Available materials and finishes are not limited to wood. Lacquered finishes, metals, and glass doors in multiple styles are also available. Hardware is heavy-duty and fully adjustable (150 lb. applied horizontally). Styles, options, and finishes are too numerous to list.	High

Figure 7.31   The rich blend of wood, stone, and warm accents creates an inviting and efficient kitchen space. *(Gayle Reynolds, ASID, IIDA. Steve Vierra Photography.)*

Table 7.2 Countertop Styles

MATERIAL	PRICE RANGE	CHARACTERISTICS
Granite, stone, stainless steel	High	Very durable; heat- and scratch-resistant; low-maintenance
Solid-surfacing material (e.g., Corian®)	High	Very durable; heat- and scratch-resistant; low to moderate maintenance
Ceramic tile	Middle to high	Very durable; heat-resistant; will have a somewhat uneven surface; may be difficult to keep grout clean
Plastic laminate	Low	Durable; however, it's best to use solid-core laminate (i.e., color extends through the thickness of the laminate) versus laminate that has color only on the surface

Figure 7.32 The striking contrast of dark cabinets against warm, gold walls gives this kitchen/dining area a casual elegance. *(Photo by Peter Paige.)*

rials, their approximate price ranges, and the durability of each. Figures 7.36 through 7.41 present excellent design ideas for small-space kitchen countertop opportunities.

Appliances for Kitchens

Your appliance selection process should include consideration of sizes, performance, finishes, and budget. (See Figure 7.42.) You may be limited on the size of a particular appliance in designing a small kitchen; however, look for appliances that are not only efficient in function, but also in size. For example, a range will take far less space than a separate cooktop and wall oven. A visit to your local appliance showrooms will reveal the vast array of size and pricing options available to suit any budget. The price ranges of appliances vary widely. There are dishwashers made to fit under an integral sink or even in the counter next to your sink, flush-profile refrigerators, and refrigerators made to go under the counter. Armed with your list of priorities and a budget, your kitchen will become a reality.

Figure 7.33 The sleek bird's-maple is contemporary in style, and it visually warms the practical stainless-steel surfacing. The rustic butcher block adds a striking textural contrast. *(Douglas Kahn/Gould Evans.)*

Figures 7.34 and 7.35 These kitchens show different looks that can be achieved through cabinetry selections. The kitchen on the left shows warm, dark cabinetry that compliments the warm hearth, antique ovens, and mosaic floor tile. The kitchen on the right utilizes light simple colors to visually brighten and simplify the space. *(Carole Harrison, Auckland Kitchens.)*

Figure 7.36 This view further demonstrates how the dining counter works in this kitchen. Whether cooking dinner, dining, or passing through, the visual warmth is a welcome respite. *(Gayle Reynolds, ASID, IIDA. Steve Vierra Photography.)*

Figure 7.37   The countertops in this kitchen incorporate the outdoors by matching the counter height with the window height. This kitchen is small and efficiently designed. The warm, complementary colors and large expanse of window view make it feel much larger. *(Gill Smith Interior and Landscape Designer, Auckland, New Zealand.)*

Figure 7.38   Granite counter surfaces contribute to the sleek contemporary design in this kitchen. The counter color has been repeated in the frames for the artwork. *(Gill Smith Interior and Landscape Designer, Auckland, New Zealand.)*

Figure 7.39 The solid surfacing material used for countertops has been fabricated to seamlessly incorporate the sink basins. Combined with the stainless-steel backsplash, this work area is a snap to clean. *(Douglas Kahn/Gould Evans.)*

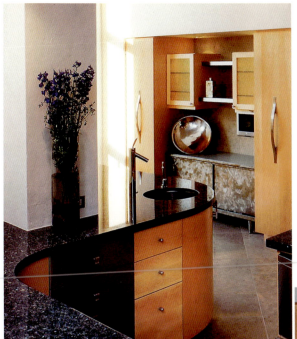

Figure 7.40 This counter has been customized to create a seamless work area. *(Lori W. Carroll, ASID, IIDA. William Lesch Photography.)*

Figure 7.41 The glass dining surface adds textural dimension to the granite surfaces. *(Lori W. Carroll, ASID, IIDA. William Lesch Photography.)*

Figure 7.42 Using tile on the back wall of a cooking area is beautiful as well as practical. Tile is a good choice for cooking areas because it's heat-resistant and easy to maintain. The finish and combination of stainless-steel appliances and ventilation hood offers the commercial kitchen look often sought by gourmet chefs and cooks alike. This illustrates how a grander-scale design look can be incorporated into a small kitchen. *(Christina Oliver. Brian Vanden Brink, Photographer, © 2002.)*

Most appliances are available in smaller-than-standard sizes—an option that provides maximum flexibility in kitchen design. For example, installing two small, under-the-counter refrigerators can provide as much storage as a standard-size refrigerator without taking up as much room.

Summary

This chapter has detailed the variations of kitchen and dining-room designs and practical considerations for small spaces, stressing the importance of careful planning and efficient design, as these spaces are likely to get more use than any other rooms and are generally more expensive to renovate. As we move out of the kitchen and on to the more personal and private rooms in your home, Chapter 8 explores how to create comfortable, restful, and beautiful bedrooms.

CHAPTER 8

Bedrooms

The bedroom is where most people spend the greatest amount of time. Surprised? Think about it: We spend an average of 10 hours a day in this room—sleeping, resting, getting ready for bed, or preparing for the day. That should be incentive enough to make the bedroom the ultimate haven to rest and renew. As with other rooms profiled in this book, we need to look at space issues that will be a challenge. Throughout this chapter, we've included work from many designers who have applied interesting, practical, and unique design solutions to the bedroom space. As with all facets of design in our own living spaces, finding the style or theme that's just right can be as simple as paying attention to how we respond to the space when we walk into it.

As we continue our journey through the home, our next stop is the bedroom. Whether your home or apartment contains one bedroom or several, you'll surely find solutions within this chapter to achieve the look you're aiming for.

In this chapter, we'll discuss the following:

- Master suites and style options for traditional, contemporary, formal, and opulent looks

- Mediterranean and tropical looks

- Cozy, restful, and restorative themes

- Children's bedrooms

Some Style Options for Master Bedrooms

When considering the bedroom(s) in a small home or apartment, think minimal. The saying "less is more" is a key component to creating a space that will allow you to relax and unwind. If the room isn't overcrowded with furniture and accessories or finished with complex palettes of color, it will have a simple, relaxed feel. Following are some effective ways to simplify your bedroom space.

- Eliminate any nonessential furnishings that cause the room to feel crowded. This can mean simply clearing away infrequently used objects or finding a storage unit that's efficiently designed. More-efficient storage units generally use vertical space and so are taller. They may also have more customized niches designed for holding specific items.

- Consider bed frames that have minimal styling and those without footboards. A full-size bed will allow more floor space in the bedroom, but if you want the queen or king size, go ahead. You can compensate by sizing down the scale or limiting the quantity of other furnishings. If you decide on the larger bed, consider making the bed and bedding the focal point of the room. This is especially effective if you're using a theme, since the bed will provide an axis that establishes the theme. Bedding is also a great way to refresh the look of the room periodically.

- Unless you're drawn to complex, highly chromatic colors, it's best to steer toward neutral, monotone palettes. As discussed in Chapter 5, "Weekend Retreats and Guest Houses," monotone color schemes calm the space and slow the pace. Monotone palettes are a collection of neutrals in the same color grouping used in graduated values and hues. Unlike monochromatic palettes that use only one hue or value of any color in varying shades or tints, monotones use neutral colors in varying shades or tints (lightness or darkness). An example of a monotone palette would be beige or grey used with varying amounts of white added to create several different values (shades or tints) of beige or grey. Many other colors can be used in monotone palettes, as long as they are neutral values or hues. Typically,

a neutral color that's not in the beige or grey color family will work best as an accent within the monotone palette. Not only will the space visually appear quieter and calmer, it will appear larger with the lighter tones.

- When accessorizing bedroom spaces, look for fabrics that have a variety of textures. This will prevent a monotone palette from looking flat or too plain. Patterns of different textures can be more effective than patterns of color because each reflects the light differently. A silk or satin material will reflect more light and will appear lighter than a velvet or chenille material of exactly the same color.

- Keep the window treatments simple. Less fabric in lighter textures will make a window look brighter and more open. If the window treatments are too dark and bulky, the room will feel closed in. If you need to have the windows fully covered at night, provide tiebacks, a traverse rod system, or light-blocking shades for nighttime use. If possible, install the curtains a few additional inches beyond the window casing so that when the curtains are opened, more of the window is exposed.

- Lighting for the bedroom can be challenging, since bedrooms typically have one utilitarian fixture centered on the ceiling and rely on lamps near the bed for additional illumination. Bedrooms should have one main light source for overall lighting, with additional task lighting as needed. In small spaces, we want to direct most of this light toward surfaces (i.e., the ceiling, walls, or art objects) because that will give the room a greater sense of space. When we focus the light sources in the center of the room, the objects within the room cast shadows along the wall, making the room feel even smaller. If the light sources in your bedroom are primarily in the center of the ceiling, and you're not able to renovate, we suggest the following solutions:

Forget the bulb on the ceiling. It doesn't do a very good job anyway.

Invest in a few torchères, which are floor lamps that direct all of their light upward. Place them in the corners to wash the ceiling with as much light as possible. While halogen lamps are generally preferred, incandescent lamps are better in the bedroom for the warm tone of light they emit. To adjust the level of light in the room, purchase torchères with three-way lightbulbs or dimming switches. When you need a full level of light, you'll have it. If you prefer a soft, gentle light level, you can have that, too.

If you have nightstands, find a couple of lamps you really love. They'll provide good reading light and can accentuate any theme or style you want. If you don't have nightstands, or don't want table lamps, consider pendants (they can be hung from hooks that are easily installed in the ceiling over the sides of the bed). The many styles of lamps and pendants available are limited only by your imagination. Note: If you decide to use pendants, try to select a style that offers diffused light or a concentrated beam of light so that it isn't overpowering when you're in bed.

If you're able to renovate or design from scratch, we suggest the following:

Determine where the circulation patterns or pathways are in the bedroom and light those walls with recessed can lights placed 6 to 12 inches from the wall to graze it with light. If you have any artwork in the room, an accent wall, or a tapestry or decorative fabric hanging on a wall, highlight it with a recessed wall washer or a low-voltage track light.

Wall sconces are a great alternative for general overall light since you can usually place them where you need them. Sconces come in a wide range of sizes and styles to suit any interior.

For more information on lighting, refer to Chapter 2, "Color and Proportion."

Some Style Options for Bedrooms

The bedroom is a great place to create a theme. Chapter 5, "Weekend Retreats and Guesthouses," explores ideas for creating the perfect place to get away from the daily chaos. Remember, a place to get away does not need to be a separate living space—it can be right in your own home. The bedroom is one of the places where we can create an oasis that will truly provide an escape from the daily grind. Explore the possibilities discussed in Chapter 5, then let your imagination be your guide.

Traditional/Historical Bedrooms

A successful traditional or historical style doesn't mean going overboard on period details. With traditional or historical style, you can simply focus on one or two details that'll set the tone. For example, if the space is of historical significance, then it's likely to already have architectural details in place. Usually, all you'll need to complement the setting will be one sensational period piece of furniture, such as a bed frame, armoire, or bombé chest of drawers. The color palette will also be important, but again, will be dependent on your own style. While the options are broad, we recommend monotone palettes in the neoclassical style, since they're light and will visually open up the space. Good neoclassical colors are pale hues of yellow, grey, beige, and ivory. Accent with layers of color of medium hue and intensity from the same color family in the drapery and upholstery fabrics, artwork, and bedding.

If the ceilings are very high, as is often the case with historical spaces, the bedroom can feel too exposed. This will be exacerbated in a small room, so if there's a picture rail, architectural moulding, or visual break in the wall that runs horizontally around the room, we recommend painting the upper part of the wall (and in some cases the ceiling) a medium hue that's a couple of shades darker than the lower part of the wall. The light color on the walls will give the room a sense of space, while the darker ceiling and upper wall area will feel more in proportion with the volume of the space. An interesting wall treatment in a traditional bedroom would be a richly colored tapestry or traditional fabric on a focal wall or centered on the wall over the bed and highlighted with an accent light.

For an opulent touch, period wall sconces and window treatments can be designed to coordinate with the style you're trying to emulate. Whether your bedroom is traditional American Colonial, French Neoclassical, Empire, or English Tudor, accessories such as sconces and window treatments will help finish the look. (See Figures 8.1 to 8.4.)

Figure 8.1 *Pale pinks enhance the traditional furnishings and accessories of this bedroom. The symmetry of the table lamps balances the space. (Photo by Peter Paige.)*

Figure 8.2 A neutral color scheme and soft textures create a nurturing ambience in this master bedroom. *(Gayle Reynolds, ASID, IIDA. Photo © Eric Roth.)*

Contemporary Bedrooms

Contemporary spaces typically have straight, clean lines and uncluttered details. In a small bedroom, this can be an advantage, where a minimalist approach to finishing and furnishing will give a greater sense of space. Options for color palettes are wide open and present the opportunity to create any style or theme you like. In a traditional bedroom, a futon's organic look may not be the right choice, but in a contemporary bedroom, it's right at home. If you prefer traditional furniture, that's okay, too. A contemporary space is similar to working with a blank canvas. One of the most common mistakes in finishing a contemporary room is to paint it entirely white or off-white. This can be very striking if the furnishings are distinctive and meant to be the focal point, but if not, it can look very flat and uninspired. To get started, we recommend choosing the palest of hues presented in the furnishings to be used in the room. Using soft, simple palettes of color will naturally enhance the room and become the

Figures 8.3 and 8.4 Elegant faux wall coverings and jacquard linens in off-white are enhanced by the very detailed use of black accents. An inviting and romantic space can be achieved with little color when details are key elements in a room. *(Maria P. Perron, Village House Interiors, LLC. Mike Rixon Photography, Bow, New Hampshire.)*

background, which will set the stage for whatever style or theme you want. (See Figures 8.5 and 8.6.)

Formal/Opulent Bedrooms

While many of the rooms that follow could easily fall into the traditional or historical genre, the addition of one or two elements can often create a truly formal or opulent space. The flowing draperies in Figure 8.7 and the added texture of the wall glazing in Figure 8.8 transform these classic bedrooms into more refined, opulent rooms. Here are other embellishments that will transform a traditional space into an opulent one:

- Dramatic accent-lighting details

- Faux wall finishes

- Distinctive artwork

- Rich fabric such as tapestry, velvet, and silk

- Well-appointed window treatments

As you can see, an opulent space is all about details. Finish the space, then add detail that takes it to another level.

Figure 8.5 Soft plums and pale greys complement the contemporary furnishings of this master bedroom. This palette is very serene and calming. *(Braun Design, Ltd., Maura Braun, IIDA. Photo © George Lambrose, Lambrose Photography, Inc.)*

Figure 8.6 This contemporary Southwestern design shows how an earth-tone palette can make a statement. The dark woven leather bed frame gives the bedroom a sense of scale. *(Lori W. Carroll, ASID, IIDA. William Lesch Photography.)*

Pay attention to the light coming into your room in the evening. The night sky often introduces a deep blue color that can be used as an accent color in your palettes.

Mediterranean and Tropical Bedrooms

Even if you do not live in a Mediterranean or tropical setting, you can create one in your bedroom. Chapter 5, "Weekend Retreats and Guest Houses," discusses

how to create these themes in detail, and Figures 8.9 through 8.11 will give you additional inspiration.

Don't be afraid to incorporate large-scale furnishings into a small room. If the room is not overfurnished, a large bed or armoire can actually give the room a greater sense of scale.

Figure 8.7 The open feeling created by the windows and high ceiling in this opulent bedroom is enhanced with the soft-flowing draperies over the four-poster bed. The use of a monochromatic palette, as in this space, creates a calming atmosphere. *(Chris Jordan, Designcorp.)*

Figure 8.8 The pale green walls, which have been glazed, set an opulent and cheerful tone for this master bedroom. *(Carol O'Brien/WDC. Photo © Stephen SetteDucatti.)*

Figure 8.9 The crisp white linens against the toile fabrics enhance the exterior Mediterranean architectural details. This is an example of how a contrasting palette can bring a contemporary flair to a traditional design. *(Gauthier-Stacy, Inc. Photographer: Sam Gray.)*

Figure 8.10 *Neutral tones blended with sunset colors of red, orange, and yellow balance this room, which includes a four-poster bed and an attractive Oriental rug. The bed, particularly, gives the room a sense of scale. (Lori W. Carroll, ASID, IIDA. William Lesch Photography.)*

Cozy Bedrooms

If your bedroom is especially small or your preference is to have it feel cozy, then color will be the first thing to consider. While we don't recommend the darkest hues for small rooms, medium hues are quite acceptable. The key is balance and proportion. If you choose a deep salsa red, then it should be balanced with some colors that are either its complement (like green) or its coordinate (like yellow).

With a darker color on the walls, the floor will appear more in proportion if it's slightly darker than the walls. A good finish to consider would be a dark hardwood like Brazilian cherry or walnut, or even a lighter wood with a darker area rug. For a cozy look, select colors from the warm side of the color wheel and layer them in varying intensities with the use of fabrics and accessories. Multilayering of color and textures will add to the coziness of a bedroom,

Figure 8.11 The tropical tones of this bedroom establish a distinct geographical identity. The palette brings the outside into the interior like a breath of fresh air. *(Arq. Diego Matthai, IIDA, Matthai Arquitectos. Photo by Sebastian Saldivar.)*

where the objective is to feel embraced by rich, warm color, softness, and visual textures. (See Figures 8.12 to 8.17.)

Restful/Restorative Bedrooms

If your goal is to create the ultimate place to retreat, rest, and restore, then incorporate as many soothing elements as possible into your bedroom. Color will be only one part of the equation. Engage as many of the senses as possible in ways that will help you connect with nature. Color palettes should be soft, soothing hues of ivory, apricot, yellow, sage green, blue-green, blue, and indigo. Wood should be intro-

duced in its natural color, since it reminds us of nature, and that makes us feel more solid, or grounded in nature. A soft scatter rug that feels good enough to lie down on will balance the solid surface of a wood floor. If you don't have a wood floor, then introduce wood or another organic material through the furnishings. Other elements that help us connect with nature are water fountains, which can be very soothing to hear, and plants. Fireplaces, if you're lucky enough to have one in your bedroom, are very comforting, but if you don't, several candles on wall sconces and on fireproof platters can have the same mesmerizing effect. Candles or potpourri can also add the sensory element of aromatherapy. Remember, it's all about

Figure 8.12 The light shades of this color palette are consistent throughout this bedroom and are used effectively in the multiple patterns and textures. *(Carol O'Brien/WDC. Photo © Stephen SetteDucatti.)*

Figure 8.13 This design demonstrates how color can create a cozy ambience for a master bedroom sitting area. The clerestory windows repeat the pattern in the window treatments. *(Carol O'Brien/WDC. Photo © Stephen SetteDucatti.)*

Figure 8.14 The French doors and the diverse shades of pink make this room a very relaxing retreat. The selection of delicate linens and accessories enhance the serene monochromatic color palette. *(Mark Woodman, CMG.)*

Figure 8.15 A cozy and spiritual bedroom is achieved through the combination of natural grass cloth on the ceiling and walls, wood flooring, and the soft-drapery-enclosed four-poster bed. *(Gauthier-Stacy, Inc. Photographer: Sam Gray.)*

Figure 8.16 This room is a getaway in space and time. The decorative lines of the wood turning on the four-poster bed enhance the Parisian style of this master bedroom. *(Andrew Liberty Interiors, IIDA.)*

Figure 8.17 Curl up with a favorite book in this cozy bedroom sitting area. The monotone finishes give this bedroom a quiet, calm feeling. The details of the furniture add a touch of style and elegance. *(Photo by Peter Paige.)*

engaging the senses of sound, sight, touch, and smell to help us connect to nature and ultimately emerge in the morning ready for a new day. (See Figures 8.18 to 8.20.)

Children's Bedrooms

A child's bedroom should be designed with the age and gender of the child in mind. Figures 8.21 through 8.25 are examples of the various styles that can be used effectively for nurseries, young children's rooms, or a teenager's space.

Practical Considerations for Children's Bedrooms

At one time, optimizing space in a child's room used to be limited to bunk beds, cubbies, and closet organizers. Today, we have a wealth of options and versatile ideas to save space and to promote greater organization. Here are some practical considerations to keep in mind:

- Finishes for a child's room need to be durable, nontoxic, and easy to clean. Expensive wallpaper may not be the best choice; choose scrubbable paint or vinyl wall covering instead.

Figure 8.18 The Eastern furniture, accessories, and the fireplace, give this bedroom a restorative radiance. The soft, recessed lighting gives the impression that the bed floats within the space. (Braun Design, Ltd., Maura Braun, IIDA. Photo © George Lambrose, Lambrose Photography, Inc.)

- A fun option for a young child's room is construction board painted with chalkboard paint on a wall area or as doors for a storage cabinet or closet.

- Floor materials such as 12-inch-square vinyl, rubber, or cork tiles give you the option of creating a fun pattern on the floor. Add a small area rug or two for comfort underfoot.

- Try adding window seats containing drawers and doors for storage. Top them with colorful pillows for reading or lounging. Size them approximately 12 to 16 inches deep and 14 to 18 inches high.

- If you have one wall or corner area, built-ins such as desk surfaces, bookshelves, and cabinets are a great space saver. If you don't want custom-built storage, there are many options for easy-to-install individual modular sections.

- With space at a premium, forgo the headboard on the bed. Instead, install decorative wainscot and mouldings, fabric, or a small mural directly on the wall as a substitute for the headboard.

- When providing storage for children, it's a good idea for some of the storage compartments to have doors. This will help keep the room clutter-free.

- Provide age-appropriate heights for storage. If a high level of storage is needed in your child's room, place items that the child will need to

Figure 8.19   This monotone palette, accented by pale blue toile fabrics and dark wood, is an example of how to achieve a restful master bedroom. *(Gauthier-Stacy, Inc. Photographer: Sam Gray.)*

Figure 8.20 The subdued monotone colors of the walls and flooring create an inviting, restful corner in this bedroom. Often, the absence of color in a space gives it a restorative quality. *(Lori W. Carroll, ASID, IIDA. William Lesch Photography.)*

Figure 8.21 This interesting view of a nursery through a mirror shows the use of a cozy window seat, designed with soft pastel shades. *(Teresa M. Burnett, Willow Designs.)*

Figure 8.22 This mural and coordinating comforter create a whimsical space for a young child. Light shades are soothing and nurturing. *(From www.tobeydesigngroup.com.)*

Figure 8.23 The soft, tranquil tones and floating draperies and fringe at the chair bottom are ideal design solutions for a young girl's room. *(Gauthier-Stacy, Inc. Photographer: Sam Gray.)*

Figure 8.24 Hats used as artwork on the wall create a feminine flair for this bedroom. The wood bed frame is contrasted with the soft cream walls and linens. *(Photo by Peter Paige.)*

access at his or her own access height, and keep items that you can reach for your child on the higher shelves.

- If more than one child shares the room, it's important that each has some individual territory. One way to accomplish this is to have a theme that allows half of the room to be painted and finished differently than the other half. Furniture doesn't need to match, and can even be used to divide the space. Bookcases make great room dividers, and you can set them up so that each side has access to half of the storage if there's not enough room to have two full back-to-back sets.

- While bedrooms are inevitably planned around the bed, don't forget to plan for other activities (e.g., a play area where the child or young adult can entertain his or her friends, storage for music/TV/computer equipment, a study area with plenty of desk space).

Children's rooms are challenging, especially because defined themes are often outgrown every few years. If you don't mind extensive redecorating as your children grow, then go ahead and have fun. Your child's room is the perfect place to bring fantasy and imagination to life. There are only a few rules to selecting color palettes in a child's room.

Figure 8.25   *The outdoor theme of this nursery is playful and nurturing. The designer has effectively used soft pastels and refreshing whites. (Maria P. Perron, Village House Interiors, LLC. Bill Fish Photography, Manchester, New Hampshire.)*

For nurseries, select any soft palette of colors that will promote a tranquil, nurturing feel, such as pale hues of blue, indigo, turquoise, green, apricot, and yellow.

In a young child's room, spend some time looking through color samples with your child. Most children have very definite likes and dislikes about color, and you should try to respect that. Unless your child selects a color that's unreasonable or impractical (black, dark brown, bright red, etc.), try to follow his or her lead. If the child insists on bright blue or some other bold saturation of color, try to find a place to view that color in a full-scale application so the child can see what it's going to look like. Sometimes children simply can't imagine a whole room painted the color that looks cool on a

little paint chip. If they persist, a compromise might be in order. Select a lighter complementary shade for the whole room and add one wall of the darker color, or install curtains, bedding, or other accents that have the darker color. Don't forget to add accents of complementary and coordinating color, and remember, whatever the outcome, they will likely outgrow the look within a few years.

The teenagers' room will likely be the last evolution of finishes you'll need to consider—at least until they move out. Young adults will have opinions about their own personal space, and unless you want a battle, it is best to go with the flow. While many young adults have a lot of stuff, many prefer the minimalist approach to finishes and furnishing. This is the good news. Many teens will try to paper their walls with posters and art, so wall color is usually not an issue. If your teen is open to suggestion, we recommend soothing, contemplative palettes selected for their simple understated feel—pale sage green, ivory, and pale gold with accents of eggplant and forest green, or perhaps pale desert sand, pale taupe, or warm grey with ivory beige trim and accents of burnt orange, periwinkle, or gold. If the overall color palette is neutral, then the accent colors will become the focal points in the room. It can be as simple as selecting a neutral palette of colors that will be a complementary background for brightly colored objects already in the room.

Summary

Your bedroom is your own private oasis. It is where you rest and renew. Ultimately, it doesn't matter if your space is traditional, contemporary, formal, or otherwise. What matters is how you feel when you're resting there. We encourage you to explore color palettes and uncover your own personal preferences. In the end, you'll have created a bedroom that does more than simply give you a place to sleep.

CHAPTER 9

Bathrooms

Until the early 1900s, the bathroom was the one room that was relegated to the outdoors. Prior to that, outhouses were commonplace, and a symbol of prestige, if you had one. Fortunately, advances with indoor plumbing have elevated the bathroom to a source of pride in the home. They've evolved from simply being a necessity in our lives to being our personal oasis in the morning and at the end of the day. We no longer simply bathe in them, we luxuriate in them. In this chapter, we'll discuss the following:

- Style options for bathrooms with emphasis on materials and finishes

- Guidelines for selection of cabinetry, countertops, fixtures, furnishings, tile, and mirrors

- Traditional, historical, and contemporary styles

As we begin our tour and review the various components of each bathroom, we'd like you to notice the way each designer has applied the basic design principles. Some are simple and minimal; some demonstrate creative uses of everyday materials; some are inspired by spas. With size considerations in mind, we say, "Make every inch count!" (See Figures 9.1 to 9.3.)

Practical Considerations for Bathrooms

Many of the principles we discussed in Chapter 8 also hold true for the bathroom. Whether the bathroom is shared, private and part of the master suite, or a simple powder room, the key components for bedrooms apply: "Less is more," and "Think minimal." Let's face it, bathrooms are already small spaces, but don't let that dissuade you from making the bathroom a space that you'll look forward to spending time in. If the bathroom is part of a master suite, you may already have an established style or theme in the bedroom that you can expand on. If it's not part of a suite, then you have the option of either continuing the style from the rest of the living space or creating a new one. The same holds true for a powder

Figure 9.1 Pale yellow tiles, walls, and fixtures provide an opportunity to introduce different color accents within the room. *(K2S Design Studio, Kathryn B. Adams and Stephanie Skovron.)*

Figure 9.2 Effective use of mirrors in this bathroom and a monochromatic palette make this bathroom a restful and elegant space. *(Carol O'Brien/WDC. Photo © Stephen SetteDucatti.)*

Figure 9.3 Architectural details created through the use of tile design add charm and distinction to this bathroom. *(Carol O'Brien/WDC. Photo © Stephen SetteDucatti.)*

room. Whatever your theme or style, color will be a big part of the equation. We've discussed color selection in each chapter, and we cannot overemphasize the importance of selecting color palettes that make you feel the most comfortable. We also encourage you to look at the color selections used in the bathrooms throughout this chapter and find one or two that resonate with you.

Here are some practical considerations to take into account:

- Think *waterproof.* Any absorbent material, such as carpet, is a poor choice for a bathroom floor.

- Wood base trim is beautiful, but if you are installing tile on the floor, consider tile for the base too. A watertight seal made between the wall and floor will eliminate potential moisture problems that are present with wood trim.

- Tile, stone, and quarry tile are excellent choices for floor and base materials; however, some of these finishes can be very slippery when wet. Select tile that's slip-resistant when wet. Check the specifications located on the back of the sample boards, or ask your flooring contractor to advise you of the rating of each tile you're considering. Any tile with a polished finish is likely to be the most slippery—wet or dry.

- As with any small space, try to develop one focal point and use the boldest colors there.

- Check your local building codes for requirements concerning electrical fixture and outlet locations.

Most municipalities require any and all electrical devices be a minimum distance from water sources such as showers, tubs, and sinks.

- Light the walls, not the space. The room will seem larger if the walls appear brighter.

Use primarily light hues in your color palettes, and don't be afraid to experiment with paint colors. As you determine the desired look for your bathroom, spend some time evaluating the type of space that makes you feel most comfortable. Ask yourself these questions:

- Do I want to simply get in and get out in the morning and at night?

- Will I use the space to relax and take time with my daily rituals?

- Do I want to feel as though I'm at the spa?

- If I install a tub, how often will I use it?

- Do I have room for a sink vanity, or will I have more room with a pedestal sink?

- What are my storage needs?

- Are there any windows?

- When I look at the room, does it already have a focal point, or is there an obvious area where I can create one?

After you've answered these few basic questions, you can then move on to the more finite issues of the bathroom design.

Materials and Finishes

With bathroom spaces, the materials and finishes you select will likely be long-term investments.

With that in mind, you'll want to choose each carefully for its life-cycle cost and durability. The only exceptions to this rule are paint on the walls and short-term items like window treatments and towels. This is where small spaces are at an advantage, because less space to finish usually means less cost. Depending on your budget and the exact size of the room, spending $5 to $10 per square foot for floor tile or marble may not be out of the question. Whatever your budget or goals for your bathroom, we recommend investing the greatest amount of money on the items that will be most expensive to replace down the road:

- *Plumbing fixtures.* Replacement of a fixture can be costly because you'll most likely need to hire a licensed plumber for the removal and installation. Toilets, sinks, tubs, showers, and faucets are not items we encourage homeowners to install or replace on their own. Changing fixtures can be challenging for various reasons. Many apartment buildings have centralized plumbing systems, and the shutoff valves may not be located in the same apartment where work is to be performed. Accessing the valves may also cause inconvenience to the tenants in adjacent apartments. It's easy to see how this can be labor-intensive, ergo expensive.

- *Structural changes.* If there's anything you'll be changing structurally in the bathroom (e.g., new walls, framing for storage or cabinetry, new window openings, relocating doors), it'll occur in the first phase of the renovation, and clearly, you'll only want to do it once.

The next layer of materials you will want to plan very carefully are the following:

- *Cabinets and counters.* If your bathroom is large enough for cabinetry or requires specialized storage, you'll need to plan this carefully. In a small bathroom, the storage considerations are more finite. Oftentimes, cabinets that must accommodate shallow clearances or that need to fit into tight spaces will need to be custom-built for the space, which is more costly. When planning for a custom cabinet, try to select one that's not so stylized or distinctive that you'll grow tired of its look. If a stylized look is what you want, then select hardware and accessories for the doors, drawers, and towel bars that can be easily changed later. Likewise, with counters. Try to keep within a style that's not likely to fall out of fashion, and dress it up with the backsplash. The backsplash will be easier to update than the counter, so spend the money on the counter first.

- *Tile and mirrors.* Tile, while it doesn't need to be expensive, will be expensive to remove if you decide you're tired of it in a few years. If you can't afford the more expensive styles, try a simple, basic tile and find a feature tile or inlay strip to dress it up. An inexpensive white ceramic tile bordered with marble inlay strips looks elegant and will have added visual texture. Good-quality mirrors can be very expensive, so size them carefully so you won't need to redo them. Unless the mirrors cover the entire wall, we recommend having them framed or decoratively edged.

- *Light fixtures.* With a very small space, as bathrooms tend to be, you won't need too many. You'll need good-quality, uniform light over the sink/makeup area and soft overall light in the rest of the room. Avoid the fan/light combination fixtures. Invest in a good-quality fan and then focus on one or two good-quality light fixtures. Once the lighting is planned properly and installed, all you'll need to change for years will be the bulbs. Please refer to earlier chapters for more detailed discussions of lighting.

- *Wall finishes and accessories.* Wall finishes are not usually very expensive. Paint will be the least expensive and is the easiest to change. Other wall finishes that involve more cost and installation skill include vinyl or paper wall coverings, paper-backed fabrics, and specialized coatings like glazing and faux finishing. Refinishing the walls, ceiling, door(s), and trim is relatively easy and inexpensive, so if you want to take a risk with the colors, do it here and it can be easily redone when you're ready for a change. Accessories are also simple to replace and can have a significant impact on the style or theme of the whole room.

As you can see, ironically, the least expensive items to redo in a bathroom are the ones that can offer the greatest visual impact. This is good news for anyone who wants to refresh the look of an existing bathroom, or anyone who lives in an apartment where there's little else you can do to redecorate.

Cabinets and Countertops

Selection of cabinetry and countertops will be one of the biggest components in determining the style or theme of your bathroom. Be creative in your selections. Cabinets can be standard, off-the-shelf varieties, or they can be custom-built to size. Finishes range from natural, stained, and painted woods to laminates, lacquers, and PVC-coated wood fiberboard. Style ranges are too numerous to list and include Colonial and Shaker styles, sleek contemporary designs, and rustic or whimsical. If you're tall, go ahead and install a kitchen-height sink base and cabinet, which are generally 6 inches higher and a few inches deeper. If you're planning on wall cabinets or wall storage, doors with glass panels will help create more visual depth, and the space will not feel as closed in. Hardware is another place where style can be expressed. Have fun with the door and drawer pulls if you want to create a unique look that is yours alone. Depending on the amount of storage needs, this is the place to take advantage of vertical storage. Less-often-used

Figure 9.4 Built-in wood cabinetry gives this traditional-style bathroom an elegant, opulent look and shows how storage space can be maximized and used to make a design statement. *(Gauthier-Stacy, Inc. Photographer: Sam Gray.)*

items can be placed on the highest shelves, while items used daily are kept within easy reach.

Countertops can be any material that is waterproof, scratch-resistant, and able to be installed horizontally. The most often used materials are plastic laminate, tile, or stone. The great thing about bathroom spaces is that there's less counter to install, so if you can't afford the expensive tile or stone surface you love in the kitchen, maybe you can afford to install it in the bathroom. In most installations, the material used on the counter is also used on the backsplash, which helps protect the wall from unnecessary water damage. The backsplash is also a good place to add detail with unique tile or tile patterns. (See Figure 9.4.)

Bathroom Fixtures and Furnishings

We don't tend to think too much about bathroom fixtures—until we need one—but being one of the most expensive components of our bathroom design, there are a few issues to consider. Bathroom fixtures and furnishings come in multitudes of colors, shapes, and sizes. If you don't have room for a vanity and sink, or if you simply want to optimize the available floor area, then a pedestal sink is a great solution. If you decide on a pedestal sink, though, be aware that you'll have less counter area to place items like toothbrush holders, cotton ball dispensers, and so forth, and you'll need to either wall-mount these items or provide a small shelf for them. Bathroom fixtures (toilets, sinks, tubs, showers, faucets, etc.), need to be selected with the following in mind:

- Size, shape, and color

- Water-saving features

- Desired style

- Overall quality and price

Figure 9.5 *Bathroom fixtures and cabinets are works of art today, and this bathroom is a good example. The delicate design of these bowl sinks makes them appear to float above the cabinets. A soft, monochromatic palette for the walls, tub, and floor give this space a restful ambience. (Gauthier-Stacy, Inc. Photographer: Greg Premru.)*

Items that fall into the bathroom-furnishings category are towel racks and toilet paper holders, accessories such as cup and toothbrush holders, window treatments, towels and linen items, bath mats, shower curtains, and miscellaneous decorative accessories. Select these items based on need, style desired, price, and color or finish. Figures 9.5 and 9.6 highlight some very distinctive fixtures, furnishings, and accessories.

Tile and Mirrors

One of the most practical investments you can make in your bathroom is to install good-quality tile and mirrors. They are both waterproof, and the durability of tile on the floor and walls is undeniable. If

Figure 9.6 *The natural color palette, unique cabinets, mirrors, and hardware create a spa-like feeling in this bathroom. The indirect lighting sources have been carefully selected to quietly wash only those surfaces that enhance the spa design. (Lori W. Carroll, ASID, IIDA. William Lesch Photography.)*

you're trying to establish a theme or particular style, mirrors make a good focal point. Different shapes, edge designs, and frame styles are available for any look you desire. Figures 9.7 through 9.10 demonstrate some effective applications.

Some Style Options for Bathrooms

Like other rooms throughout a living space, style options for the bathroom are nearly unlimited. In the following sections, we discuss a few of the basic styles that we've covered throughout the book.

Traditional/Historical Bathrooms

As we mentioned at the beginning of this chapter, it wasn't until the early 1900s that inside plumbing and bathrooms came along. When this happened, existing structures needed to have this plumbing added on, usually in a room that was adjacent to the bedroom area. This is one reason that bathrooms in very old houses are often quite large in contrast to later-twentieth-century homes and apartments. The room, prior to becoming a bathroom, may have been a sitting area, a nursery, a storage room, or a small bedroom. When the fixtures were added, the

Figure 9.7 A sense of openness is achieved in this bathroom with the creative use of mirrors. The granite countertop appears to be much larger due to the placement of the mirrored wall. *(Braun Design, Ltd., Maura Braun, IIDA. Photo © George Lambrose, Lambrose Photography, Inc.)*

Figure 9.8 *The repetitive reflections maximize this space. The off-white palette and vanity add to this design concept. (Gauthier-Stacy, Inc. Photographer: Sam Gray.)*

plumbing could not be buried in the floor or walls, but rather was installed on the surface. Many tubs and toilets were installed on raised platforms that housed the pipes. Sometimes whole floors and the walls in one part of the room were covered in tile so that a showerhead could be used. These are all considerations to remember if your intent is to create a traditional or historical bathroom. (See Figures 9.11 and 9.12.) If you don't want to include the less practical aspects of an authentic style, then look to the classic traditional styles of fixtures to do the job. Key elements to complete the look include the following:

- Use a floor material that might have been available during the era you're trying to emulate. Depending on the period in history, large marble or travertine tile (12 × 12 inches or 12 × 24 inches) or small (1-square) porcelain or ceramic mosaics might work. Other options are wood, linoleum, and Mexican tile.

- Walls often had wood wainscot (usually painted), ceramic tile, or stone tile (e.g., marble, slate, or travertine). When selecting paint colors, keep this in mind, because neoclassical architecture used paint colors that emulated marble and stone

Figure 9.9 The artwork embellishes the design of this bathroom by complementing the sea-foam green tiles and glass-block details. This is an excellent example of a color palette for tranquility. *(Christina Oliver. Brian Vanden Brink, Photographer, © 2002.)*

Figure 9.10 The combination of mirrors, slate, and ebony-finished wood give this bathroom a textural, exotic look. *(Gayle Reynolds, ASID, IIDA. Photo © Eric Roth.)*

from the Gothic and Greek architecture styles. If you're simply painting the walls, consider glazing or faux finishing or vinyl wallpaper that will successfully represent your style. Another option is to use two or three pale hues of the neoclassical colors throughout the room. Try combining ivory with pale hues of grey, yellow, or apricot. You can add darker intensities of these colors with the accessories.

- Light fixtures come in many traditional and historically correct styles. For authenticity, stay with sconces and small pendants.

- Finally, if there's room, incorporate a small piece of furniture that would have been around during the period your style reflects. A small chair, a floor or wall cabinet, or a lamp table can add appreciable charm to the look.

Figure 9.11 This designer achieves classic style with architectural details and interior elements that create harmony and balance. (Braun Design, Ltd., Maura Braun, IIDA. Photo © George Lambrose, Lambrose Photography, Inc.)

Figure 9.12 *A neutral, neoclassical-inspired color palette combines with elegant pedestal sinks and a marble fireplace surround to enhance the architectural details in this traditional bathroom. (Bennet Phillips, Phillips Design Resources, Inc.)*

Contemporary Bathrooms

A contemporary-style bathroom has very few rules. The style is efficient and straightforward, and the look can range from antiseptic to colorful and whimsical. When finishing a contemporary bathroom, the following elements will be important to complement the design:

- Choose sleek styles of accessories that incorporate various textures such as metals and painted and lacquered finishes.

- Floor materials can include most ceramic, porcelain, and quarry tile in classic colors like white, black, primaries, and any other solid color, as well as natural wood or stone.

- Colors can be from any palette you like; however, with a small room, avoid the darkest hues and saturation. Consider an all-white background with chromatic accents such as red, yellow, blue, or black.

- Light fixtures can be recessed fixtures with small 3½-inch apertures located close to the walls so they graze or wash the wall surface, lighting the wall. Another option is to add contemporary-style track lights with small, low-voltage lamps to direct the light wherever you want it. There are enormous numbers of light fixture styles to select from.

- Last, the accessories can make all the difference. If the fixtures, cabinets, countertops, walls, and floor are all simple, then the hardware, accessories, artwork, and linens will define the look.

One of the greatest aspects of contemporary design in the bathroom is its efficiency. It is uncluttered, the storage is well organized, and the look will work well in almost any bathroom space. For a small space, this minimal style is a very good choice. (See Figures 9.13 to 9.16.)

Figure 9.13 *Window treatments and accessories bring character and restfulness to this contemporary bathroom. This design represents the versatility of a contrasting color palette. (K2S Design Studio, Kathryn B. Adams and Stephanie Skovron.)*

Figure 9.14 Mirrors add depth and illusion to this bathroom, creating a spa-like design. The applied tiles bring architectural detail and interest into the space. *(Gauthier-Stacy, Inc. Photographer: Sam Gray.)*

Figure 9.15 The contemporary design of this bathroom is achieved with the wood, pedestal sink, and natural tiles, which create a rich and holistic appeal. *(Christina Oliver. Brian Vanden Brink, Photographer © 2002.)*

Figure 9.16 The small exterior niche becomes an extension of this bathroom and adds a spa-like feel to the space. *(Lori W. Carroll, ASID, IIDA. William Lesch Photography.)*

Summary

As with the bedroom, your bathroom can become your own private oasis. Spending a little extra time planning the space will pay off by giving you a bathroom that's as durable and efficient as it is beautiful.

CHAPTER 10
Home Offices

With the trend toward working from home evolving rapidly, we want to offer some parameters and design ideas to assist and guide you in creating a beautiful home office that functions well. This chapter will outline the following:

- Practical considerations for home offices

- Style options for traditional/historical, contemporary, formal/opulent, and eclectic spaces

Since small living spaces need to use every part of a space to its greatest advantage, a home office is likely to double as a den for television viewing or a guest bedroom. Often, the room originally was intended to be a small bedroom or guest room. With a little creativity and efficiency, you can have a home office that is efficient, practical, and multifunctional.

Practical Considerations for Home Offices

As you plan your home office, here are some questions you'll want to ask yourself:

- Will I be using this space as my full-time office, or will I work in this space for only a few hours of my workweek?

- Will I need to meet with clients in this space? If so, is there an appropriate place for me to do this?

- Is the lighting adequate?

- What electronic equipment will I need?

    Telephone. Will I need a separate line for business and another for the facsimile machine and the computer?

    Computer. Desktop or laptop?

Printer. Inkjet or laser?

Photocopier. Desktop or floor model?

- How much horizontal desk space do I need?

- How much storage will I require?

- Will the room also be used as a guest room or family den? If so, there will be additional furniture and storage considerations?

  Will a sleep sofa be included?

  Will there be a built-in storage/media cabinet for a television and audio system?

  Can the office function be easily cleared so that the room can be used for other purposes?

Keep in mind that laser printers use more amperage than inkjet printers, and floor-model copiers use more amps than desktop types, so check with a licensed electrician before installing office equipment to determine whether you have enough room on the circuit in your home office space.

After you've considered these issues, it'll be easier to plan the layout of your space. Start by looking at the overall room, evaluating the perimeter, outlet, cable, and phone line locations and window and door locations. While there may be several options for desk/workspace location, some small spaces can be limited. There may be only one corner that allows you to fully use the space, which would preclude the option of placing the desk in the center of the room, for example.

Once you've established the location of your primary workspace in the room, you can begin to look at the lighting issues. Oftentimes, small office spaces need no more than the addition of a desk lamp and a fixture that can be mounted under an overhead storage cabinet for task light. If the additional demand is greater than that, you'll need to consult with a licensed electrician.

When providing light for a home office, don't overdo it. Keep the overall light level soft and add task light where you need it.

Color for your home office or multiuse space can be very flexible. Office spaces tend to be white, off-white, and neutral color palettes, which are perfectly suited for a straightforward professional office environment. The advantage to the home office is the ability to paint and accessorize any way you want. Start by looking at what you have. If the furnishings are all of the same style and allow you to work with minimal clutter, then a simple, neutral color palette is in order so the furnishings can take center stage; if the furniture and accessories are eclectic or of various styles, then a bolder color on the walls will help de-emphasize the unmatched furnishings. We'll discuss color palettes in more detail in each style section.

Where other rooms call for color palettes that are neutral and restful, the home office is a good place to favor palettes that stimulate and inspire.

Some Style Options for Home Offices

Aside from whether your home office is traditional, historical, contemporary, or eclectic, you'll want to consider how the space will be used. If the space is to function as home office and guest room, home office and family room, or all three, the furnishings will need additional planning. It's a good idea to keep the office workspace organized so the work function can easily be put away or disguised and not overlap the sitting or sleeping area. Fortunately, there are many attractive options for bedding, such as sleep sofas and chairs, futons, Murphy beds, and daybeds (with and without trundles). Wall storage and entertainment units can be cleverly designed to include custom niches to house televisions, VCRs, audio equipment, computer printers or fax machines, file drawers, and miscellaneous storage for tapes, CDs, office supplies, bedding, and other items. Regardless of whether the room is being used for office, sleeping, or entertaining, sleep sofas and built-in wall storage are very practical options for any small space.

Traditional/Historical Home Office Spaces

Traditional and historical spaces are uniquely challenging because they usually have very little unbroken wall area for furniture layout, and unless the wiring has been upgraded, there may not be enough room on the existing circuit.

Before consulting with a licensed electrician, make a complete list of all electrical fixtures and equipment to determine your total electrical requirement.

Another challenge to traditional and historical spaces is higher ceilings, which make lighting more difficult. Track light is a practical solution because it will allow as much light as you need and can be directed wherever you need it. Track lighting can also have its track suspended below the ceiling instead of mounted directly on the ceiling surface, similar to a pendant light. As with any small space, light the wall surfaces and ceiling wherever possible to create a greater sense of spaciousness. If the room is also used as a family room or guest room, then the light for viewing television or relaxing will be less distracting with indirect light. Window treatments such as light-diffusing pull-down shades should be considered to allow for glare control to shield computer screens during the brightest times of the day. (See Figures 10.1 and 10.2.)

Figure 10.1 Traditional furnishings and artwork bring an elegant character to this study. The subdued palette promotes thought and concentration for reading and writing. *(Photo by Peter Paige.)*

Figure 10.2 *The designer has captured true traditional style for this home office. Warm gold and red tones enhance the wood furnishings. Lighting is very subtle, yet effective for this setting. (Braun Design, Ltd., Maura Braun, IIDA. Photo © George Lambrose, Lambrose Photography, Inc.)*

Be sure to include dimming controls for the light fixtures so you can adjust the lighting level for each function of the room.

Contemporary Home Office Spaces

Contemporary spaces are possibly the easiest for designing a home office or multifunction space. The walls are likely to be smooth and even, with electrical outlets located at regular intervals for plugging in office equipment. Newer spaces are also likely to

have cable ports and phone lines already in place, which will make it much easier to install office and computer equipment. While it isn't a hard-and-fast rule, contemporary spaces can be more conducive to multiple functions than traditional spaces because of the clean, unbroken lines of the design, which allows a more even, efficient layout of various furniture items. (See Figures 10.3 and 10.4.)

Color options for contemporary spaces are similar to those for any style of space. Where there tends to be little to no architectural detailing, it's a good idea to bring accent color into the space through

Figure 10.3 This contemporary design solution provides contrast and maximizes the storage capacity for this home office. Creative lighting adds a touch of sparkle to the room perimeter. *(Gayle Reynolds, ASID, IIDA. Steve Vierra Photography.)*

artwork or colorful storage units, while keeping the wall areas neutral or lighter tones. By doing this, the artwork becomes the detail. (See Figure 10.5.)

Figure 10.6 shows that a home workspace doesn't have to be a room by itself. If the space is an open-plan design, a storage wall that doubles as a room divider is an excellent way to create separation of space to enable you to get some work done.

Formal/Opulent Home Office Spaces

If the space you're designing is formal or opulent, you'll want to pay close attention to how you furnish

Figure 10.4 Timeless design is the emphasis of this home office. The granite top on the desk is an upscale design solution. *(Christina Oliver. Brian Vanden Brink, Photographer © 2002.)*

Figure 10.5 The ceiling design is an innovative way to bring color and scale to a space. The lighting, painted shelves, and stained glass further reflect the imaginative design of this space. *(Mark Woodman, CMG.)*

Figure 10.6 This home office shows one way to divide space, serving as a work area and a media center for the home. *(Douglas Kahn/Gould Evans.)*

it. As we've discussed throughout this book, formal/opulent design is exemplified by the addition of one or more details that make a space appear more formal or opulent. In home office design, starting with a well-appointed space having classic colors and finishes, as portrayed in Figure 10.7, will achieve a formal look. The office furniture is then selected from styles that coordinate with the space and, as with any formal or opulent space, add the extra detail. Extra details include fully coordinated styles of desks, storage units, seating, and desk accessories. Items that don't match or coordinate will look out of place in a formal or opulent space. If other functions are to occur in this room, such as sleeping or entertaining, then any furnishings related to these functions will also need to coordinate with the office furniture. Lighting should be soft and elegant, using wall sconces, wall grazing and accent light (with recessed can lights), and coordinating desk lamps for added task light.

Eclectic Home Office Spaces

Eclectic home office spaces offer the most flexibility in color, design, and furnishings—the furniture doesn't have to match in an eclectic space. (See Figures 10.8 to 10.10.) For small spaces, you'll want to consider the following:

Figure 10.7 *Individual style and opulence describe this detailed home office. The wooden window seat and window surround warm the workspace. The designer has provided storage efficiency through the workstation. (Braun Design, Ltd., Maura Braun, IIDA. Photo © George Lambrose, Lambrose Photography, Inc.)*

- If the space is already eclectic without being furnished, keep most of the office furniture simple and uncluttered. This is the place to highlight a single piece of office furniture or equipment such as an antique object. If the rest of the furniture is simple, the highlighted object will stand out more.

- If the space is of a style that doesn't match your preference, then try painting colors that are not typical of that style, but rather are more in line with your own liking. Then furnish the space with additional items that more closely reflect your own style.

- As with any small space, install furnishings that will serve more than one purpose (built-in storage walls, sleep sofas, a table desk that can double as a game table when not being used for office work, etc.).

Figure 10.8 Eclectic diversity with a timeless design describes this elegant office space. A neutral color scheme allows the fine collectibles to be accents for the room. *(Braun Design, Ltd., Maura Braun, IIDA. Photo © George Lambrose, Lambrose Photography, Inc.)*

Figure 10.9 The designer has created a small home office area, wrapping the space in natural wood tones. This helps to expand the office, allowing the books, the chair upholstery, and the area rug to bring color accents to the room. *(Gayle Reynolds, ASID, IIDA. Photo by Sam Gray.)*

Figure 10.10 Contemporary chic is the essence of this home office design. The black furniture, the artwork, and the plantings bring accents of style to the room. *(Lori W. Carroll, ASID, IIDA. William Lesch Photography.)*

As discussed under "Practical Considerations for Home Offices" earlier in this chapter, a space that serves more than one function benefits from efficient storage. Whether the storage is for a television, games, audio equipment, office supplies, bedding, or refreshments for entertaining, it's a good idea to have most of it concealed by doors to maintain a less cluttered appearance. (See Figure 10.11.)

Summary

This chapter has outlined several practical solutions to the home office dilemma, regardless of your individual needs. Once you've addressed the parameters outlined under "Practical Considerations for Home Offices," you can apply your own unique criteria to your workspace. As home workspaces continue to evolve, look to technology for items that will perform multitasks and be smaller and more efficient as well. While it used to be a luxury to have a den or a place to do office work or paperwork at home, it's now a necessity for many of us. Whether you actually need a home workspace or simply would like one, it makes sense to plan for your needs ahead of time.

Figure 10.11 Built-in storage allows this multifunction space to fill many needs while occupying a small amount of square footage. *(Arq. Diego Matthai, IIDA, Matthai Arquitectos. Photo by Sebastian Saldivar.)*

APPENDIX

Guidelines for Getting Started

This appendix will guide you through the organizational process needed to successfully complete your project. We'll explain how to get started and organized, then outline the following:

- Personalizing a small space

- Incorporating what you've got

- Using color for design flexibility

- Budget considerations

- Hiring contractors

- Executing and completing the project with information on

    Scheduling

    Working in phases

    Doing it yourself

When working with color, we advise clients to spend some time with the space(s) for which they're selecting a palette. Look at the light, textures, function, size, and shape of the room. It can take time for this process to unfold, so be patient. Start with one design element at a time until you feel more comfortable with the ambience you're creating. You may want to start with a fresh coat of paint, or perhaps some new floor finishes or window treatments. Where to start will depend on the overall amount of design changes you anticipate doing. As you introduce each new element to your space, ask yourself whether it genuinely adds to the overall look you're trying to achieve. If it doesn't enrich the ambience, then try something else. And remember, in the words of the great modern architect Ludwig Mies van der Rohe, "Less is more." (See Figures A.1 and A.2.)

Getting Organized

The first step toward achieving the look you want is to get organized. As you shop, keep a list handy of things you need and like, as well as the following information and materials:

- Sample photos of rooms that have the look you're trying to achieve. Magazines are a great resource for this. In addition to being helpful with the overall look, they can be useful tools for finding interesting color combinations. Cut out or photocopy samples of anything that appeals to you, whether or not the look and colors work with other rooms in your home.

- A listing of resources where you can find further inspiration, such as paint, fabric, and furniture stores, building and lighting fixture centers, architects, and interior designers.

- After you've selected them, samples of the paint, fabrics, wall coverings, tile, wood, and flooring. We recommend selecting the flooring first, since this is the most difficult element to change.

- A sketch and photo of the room(s) you'll be working on. The sketches and photos are a valuable tool for conveying the existing condition of the room(s) to contractors and salespeople.

Figure A.1 In this particular home, the designer has maintained a soft, neutral palette of warm colors so that the owner's art collection becomes the focal point. The seating and congregating furnishings are then the only other additions of strong color, which allows for more long-term versatility. *(Gill Smith, Interior and Landscape Designer, Auckland, New Zealand.)*

Personalizing a Small Space

When it comes to personalizing a space, there are three perspectives to consider: the function of the space, the style that you want to achieve, and how to incorporate what you've already got, such as collectibles, artwork, pottery, furniture, and area rugs.

1. *Function.* How you use a space is a key consideration when designing a room. Some people prefer basic, minimalist bathrooms, while others enjoy all the accoutrements of a spa. One person may want a real chef's kitchen, while another may prefer to keep the kitchen basic and utilitarian. Do you have a kitchen/dining room or a kitchen with an adjacent sitting area or family room? The list of potential functions is enormous, so you need to focus first on the ways in which you'll be using the space.

2. *Style.* As we've discussed throughout the book, there are a tremendous number of styles to choose from, including traditional, contemporary, formal, and eclectic. You can also look to the geographical location of your space for

Figure A.2 The saturated blue used on the upper part of these walls balances the abundance of painted wood and high ceilings. The large amount of wood casework in this room could become overpowering if it were stained or painted in a dark color. *(Treena Crochet, A Matter of Style, Ltd. Photo © Stephen SetteDucatti.)*

clues on a style. Your choice of style will influence the wall, floor, and window treatments, furniture, color palette, and lighting selections, so it will have a significant impact on how the space is personalized.

3. *Incorporating what you've got.* Your collectibles, family photos, artwork, and other belongings are the ways in which you truly personalize a space. When choosing a style and color palette, consider the types of personal touches you'll want to put into the space. For example, if you're planning to display a collection of pottery in the room,

select a color palette that plays up the colors in the pottery; if you've got a substantial art collection already framed in a traditional style, you might want to think twice before you choose a contemporary style for the space. (See Figures A.3 and A.4.)

> *Personalizing a space sometimes requires thinking outside of the box, but in the end, you'll have a room that's as individual as you are. (See Figure A.5.)*

Figure A.3   *You can personalize a space with color, texture, unique furnishings, bold fabrics, and accessories. (Lori W. Carroll, ASID, IIDA. William Lesch Photography.)*

Figure A.4 The addition of a single sculptural element can completely transform the space and give it a personality of its own.
(Mike Sinclair/Gould Evans.)

Figure A.5 By reversing established principles of color use in design, this bedroom has become very personalized. Typically, the walls, floors, and other hard surfaces would be neutral, leaving the addition of richer hues to the window treatments, bedding, and so forth. This is a most dramatic effect. (Tom Gass, IIDA, Gass Design. Photo by Peter Paige.)

Using Color for Design Flexibility

When designing a space and the use of color in that space, it's important to consider the elements that are fixed in place or not easily changed, such as wall-to-wall carpet, wallpaper, and built-in cabinetry. These are the elements of a space that are not easily changed without incurring substantial costs and disruptions. The flexible items in a space are elements such as accessories (e.g., the collectibles discussed earlier in this appendix), slipcovers, and accent pillows and fabrics. The flexible elements are those that allow you to easily rotate a light color palette to a darker one for seasonal variety, for example. As long as the hard finishes such as the carpet, paint, and wall finishes are neutral, you'll be able to maintain maximum flexibility with color changes.

Remember, even paint, wall covering, and floor finishes need to be changed periodically. Depending on the quality of these materials, they should be changed every 5 to 10 years. Long-term finishes such as hardwood floors, stone, tile, marble, and granite will stand the test of time for many more years, so be mindful of this when selecting these finish materials. Organic colors are the safest bet with long-term finishes, as they can be nicely accented with a wide variety of color palettes, thereby giving you maximum flexibility for updating a room's look later.

Budget Considerations

Budget considerations are a key part of successfully planning a design project. Start by creating a list of all aspects of the project, including details such as square footage. Once you've determined the scope of work, you can begin to set a realistic budget and timeline for completion. The timeline, also known as a *critical path method* (CPM), will enable you to maintain focus on the completion schedules, resources, and money allotted for each phase. A timeline will lay out the project on a chart similar to a calendar showing the dates that different parts or phases of the project will begin and end, deadlines for selecting materials and hiring contractors, and overlap of different functions. Included with the timeline will be lists of contractors, permits needed, and any contact phone numbers, as well as a breakdown of costs for building materials, labor, permits, fees, and miscellaneous expenses and contingencies. (A *contingency* is a percentage based on the total cost of materials and labor that allows for unforeseen or unplanned expenses.) Most contingencies range from 10 to 20 percent, but will vary depending on the size and scope of the project and your geographical location. As discussed in Chapter 3, different materials and labor costs can vary from one geographical location to another, so it's beneficial to speak directly with your own local suppliers and contractors. The most important reason for having a timeline, or CPM, is to keep track of the different trades or functions needing to be completed before other trades or functions can begin. For example, in an extensive renovation requiring several trades, you want to schedule Sheetrock (also known as gypsum wallboard) to be installed and finished *after* the wiring and plumbing is completed. And you'd schedule painting or wallpapering *after* the Sheetrock is installed, taped, and finished. This may require some discipline at first, but when the finished product starts unfolding, you'll be pleased with the results of careful planning.

When creating your list of all aspects of the project, identify the major renovations to be done. Without proper planning, the major renovations can result in costly and unnecessary delays. If you're not a licensed professional, you'll need the assistance of an experienced building inspector, contractor, architect, or designer who is well versed with code, zoning, and occupancy issues in your area. If you can't pass the necessary inspections to secure an occupancy permit, all other work you do will be to no avail. Even if the space was up to code prior to your renovations, some municipalities require you to upgrade everything to meet current building codes if your renovation exceeds a certain dollar figure. Types of issues that may be of concern would include safety of electrical and plumbing systems, structural integrity, stair tread width, height and depth, mechanical systems, and proper disposal of demolition and construction materials.

If the project will be extensive and involve more than one room, it may be a good idea to perform the work in phases. Working in phases can sometimes allow you to adhere more carefully to your budget.

The next section of this appendix discusses the potential advantages and disadvantages of working in phases.

Remember, if you're not experienced with building or renovation, consulting with a licensed professional will give you valuable insight into the process and help you to determine whether phasing the project is in your best interest.

A project budget should take the following considerations into account:

- Fees for consultants, architects, engineers, interior design, or decorating services.

- General construction costs, including demolition, new construction, HVAC (heating, ventilating, air-conditioning), electrical (including new light fixtures), plumbing, finish cabinetry, trim, and painting.

- Finish materials, including installation fees where applicable.

  Wall finishes not already included in painting

  Floor materials

  Window treatments

  Light fixtures (freestanding)

  Furniture

  Accessories

  Artwork

- Contingencies, which are allowances for the possibility of cost increases during the course of a project. Contingencies are generally based on a percentage (usually from 10 to 20 percent) of the total estimated construction cost.

- Insurance and permit fees, if required.

Executing and Completing the Project

Once the budget is established for the project, you'll need to determine the specifics for the execution and the completion of the job. You'll have to decide whether to do the work yourself or hire contractors or artisans. You may decide to do a portion of the work yourself and to subcontract for the more specialized aspects.

If the job is complex and involves several overlapping specialties, it's a good idea to find a reliable general contractor. Most have their own crews of plumbers, HVAC contractors, electricians, rough and finish carpenters, cabinetmakers, drywall installers, painters, flooring contractors, and miscellaneous suppliers. A good general contractor will be able to line up all of the subcontractors, order building materials and supplies, and interface with each trade to get the job done efficiently. Contractors are also familiar with local codes, permits, and required licenses.

If time isn't a factor, or the job is relatively simple (new paint, wall covering, new floor finishes, or decorating accessories), it can be very rewarding to do it yourself.

Scheduling

Whether hiring a contractor or completing the work on your own, a realistic schedule and a process to manage the work needs to be established at the beginning. To ensure realistic expectations, include time for order and delivery of materials in your schedule. If you're ordering materials yourself that contractors will need to do their job, it's especially vital to know exactly when materials will be delivered. You don't want your electrical contractor to show up to install light fixtures that haven't arrived, or a crew of finish contractors waiting around for a cabinet delivery!

Additional time should also be factored in for potential errors with manufacturing and shipments, especially if you're ordering custom work or furniture. Often, modifications or changes can occur while the renovation work is in progress, and it's important to plan for this possibility early on.

Working in Phases

Depending on the cost and complexity of the work, doing the work in phases may be a good option.

Potential advantages to working in phases include the following:

- The work is completed as it can be afforded, making it easier to stick to your original budget.

- If the areas to be renovated are separate, phases will minimize inconveniences.

- Working in phases allows you to live with gradual changes, thus helping you more clearly define the later portions of the renovation.

- Because it's a slower process, working in phases can give you some flexibility in determining which parts of the process you'd be comfortable doing yourself and which parts are better left in the hands of experienced professionals. At the outset of a project, for example, you're likely to be more optimistic about your abilities. After actually doing the work, you may find that it's considerably more difficult and time-consuming than you thought, and you'll want to leave more aspects to professionals than you'd originally planned.

Potential disadvantages of working in phases include the following:

- The overall renovation will likely extend over a longer period of time.

- Since not all contractors are willing to accept small jobs, a limited selection of contractors may available to you.

- Economies of scale are lost. Sometimes there are savings on bulk purchases of materials, and contractors have to spend approximately the same amount of time setting up for a small project as they do for a large project.

- Occasionally, renovation in one area causes the need for renovation in an adjacent area. This falls into the category of unforeseen expense. For example, the contractor has started demolition work and finds that floor heights in adjacent rooms are not aligned or that there's been a moisture problem hidden behind a wall that is now exposed. These are examples of conditions that will require additional work outside the scope of the original contract.

Doing It Yourself

If you choose to do the work yourself, you'll want to get organized right away to ensure that you don't forget critical components of the project. Once you've researched the scope of the work and the budget, the next step is to make a preliminary checklist. This list serves several purposes: (1) to outline each aspect of the project, (2) to help prioritize tasks, and (3) to eventually become your to-do list. Following is an example of the evaluation questions we'd ask to prepare a preliminary checklist for a project:

Exterior

What does the exterior look like?

- Does it need paint?

- Does it need trim replacement or repair?

- Are there any worn stairs, decking, or handrails?

- Are the windows in reasonable shape with regard to glazing, caulking, storm windows, shutters, or insect screens?

Interior

FLOORING

- What are the floor coverings (or, more important, what is the substrate)?

  Hardwood

  Carpet

  Tile or stone

  Sheet vinyl or linoleum

WALL COVERINGS

- What is the condition of the walls?

  Good, but bad color or wallpaper

  Good, but in need of color or texture

  Plaster, wood, or paneling

  Damaged

- Is there any decorative moulding or trim? Is it worth preserving?

USAGE AND FUNCTION

- Is the space being fully used, or is there wasted space?

LIGHTING

- What type of lighting is there?

- What is the potential to alter the amount and location of fixtures?

- How much natural daylight will be available based on window sizes, location, and geographic orientation?

- If recessed fixtures or wall sconces are desired, how easily can this be done?

An electrical contractor will be able to give a fair assessment of the condition of the electrical system as well as its potential for changes. This will all be based on the electrical capacity wired into the structure. If the renovation is expansive electrically, then additional circuits may be needed.

PLUMBING

- How many fixtures are in place?

  ☐ Number of toilets

  ☐ Number of sinks

  ☐ Lavatory

  ☐ Utility sink

  ☐ Kitchen

The condition of the existing plumbing is of obvious importance. Again, a thorough assessment by a licensed plumbing contractor will be necessary to determine whether alterations are needed. At this point in the process, you may be able to determine only what you have, where the fixtures are located, and how many are needed.

Once you've done your evaluation, the preliminary checklist will naturally evolve into a detailed, prioritized checklist of things that need to be done. To stay as organized as possible, create a list of contractors, subcontractors, suppliers, municipal officials, and other related contacts along with their addresses and phone numbers and attach it to your preliminary evaluation and checklist. Also, keep track of prices and bids as you collect them so that all of your critical information is organized and handy. We find that for larger-scale renovations, archive or banker boxes make good organizers because you're also likely to collect many brochures, catalogs, color chips, swatches, and samples. If you start out organized, you're more likely to stay organized and not lose track of important details.

Hiring Contractors

When hiring contractors and artisans to execute the work—and we cannot stress this strongly enough—*get references and recommendations.* Following are some good resources for beginning your search for a contractor:

- Check with your local code-enforcement officer and ask for recommendations.

- Look in the phone book.

- Search the Internet.

Talk to at least three different contractors. Following are some questions to ask when interviewing contractors:

- Do you have room in your schedule to accommodate my project?

- When can you start, and how long will it take?

- Can you give me an estimate of cost?

- If the project is well defined, ask for a firm bid or a not-to-exceed amount.

- Can you give me references? You should *always call* the reference(s) and ask the following questions:

  Was the job completed on time?

  Was it within budget?

  Was the contractor flexible and fair with any unforeseen changes or requests?

Were there any problems?

Did the on-site crews keep the work area as safe and clean as possible?

Are you pleased with the result?

Would you use this contractor again?

- If several trades will be involved, do they have their own crews, a select list of subcontractors, or do they use whomever is available?

- If finish work is a priority in the project, do they have their own millwork or cabinet shop?

- Do they have insurance?

- If you've been given a bid, ask for it in writing (including contingencies and qualifications), and ask that it be dated.

- Once you receive a bid in writing, check to be sure the contractor has outlined exactly what you are and are not getting for the price indicated. If it isn't in writing, don't assume it will be done! Clarity at the beginning of the project will save frazzled nerves later in the process.

After you've evaluated all of your options, consulted with references, and feel comfortable with one or more contractors, you can make an informed decision. Although this can take some time, it's an invaluable part of the process. This planning stage and attention to detail will carry you through the project as easily as possible.

Summary

Throughout this book, we've introduced you to the principles of color, how and why we seem to be affected by color, and practical considerations for its use. We've guided you through the application of color in studio and loft spaces, guesthouses and retreats, and every room in the home from the entry to the bedroom. This appendix has outlined the process of how to get your project started and how to bring it to completion, whether you're doing it yourself or hiring a contractor. Regardless of the size and location of your space, the goal is to create an environment that's comfortable and pleasing to you. By starting with what you know, using this book as a guide, and adding design elements you like, ultimately, you'll end up with a living space that's uniquely yours.

BIBLIOGRAPHY

Barnes, Christine, *Color for Your Home,* Sunset Publishing Corp., Menlo Park, CA, 1999.

Birren, Faber, *Color & Human Response,* John Wiley & Sons, New York, 1978.

Eiseman, Leatrice, *Colors for Your Every Mood,* Capital Books, Inc., Sterling, VA, 1998.

Gage, John, *Color & Meaning,* University of California Press, Berkeley and Los Angeles, CA, 1999.

Pile, John, *Interior Design,* Harry N. Abrams Publishers, New York, 1988.

Whiton, Sherrill, *Interior Design & Decoration,* J.B. Lippencott Company, Philadelphia, 1974.